Leadership Toolbox for Project Managers

Achieve better results in a dynamic world

–

Michel A. Dion, PMP

Visit Project-Aria, my website on project management,
for more information:

www.project-aria.ca

I would like to dedicate this book to Valérie Gaudreault, my beautiful wife, my inspiration, for her support, and the gift of our two sons, Tristan and Mathias.

Overview of the book

The inspiration for this book

Life takes us on many different paths. This book is inspired by two of the paths I have travelled in the past years of my life: discovering project management and studying leadership. Both of these can transform your life and help you achieve new, bigger goals. They expand the frontier of what you think you can do.

I started my career in the early 90s with jobs in the banking sector. It was interesting, as I liked finance, but it was also a bit of the same thing every workday. I then became a CPA, CGA in Canada and was exposed to working on a project basis. Throughout my career, I managed various projects, mostly on the business and accounting side. This exposure to projects was more an accident of life than a career plan, but it was perfect for me. I always loved working on projects, especially special initiatives or urgent projects. I like to say that usually, when offered a project, people are wise enough to ask questions first and then say *"no,"* but I tend to say *"yes"* and then ask questions later. By then, it is usually too late to decline, and I have to find a solution.

The newer and more complex the projects were, the better they were for me. I always love to discover and explore new things, and projects fit that passion. My mind is forever curious, and I am always seeking out new adventures for my life and my mind. I tend to get bored with the monotony of repeating the same things over and over. My passions tend to be infinite learning experiences, such as music and chess, which can never be completely mastered. Who can say that they completely mastered music? Like Russian composer Sergei Rachmaninov (1873-1943[1]) said, *"Music is enough for a lifetime, but a lifetime is not enough for music.[2]"* That is probably why music has always been a part of my life: music has infinite space for creativity.

My favorite part of music has always been composition. Many musicians have ideas; very few can compose and transform their ideas into a new piece of music. I love the challenge of moving from a blank page to composing a highly complex and interesting piece of music. It is such a pleasure. Project management and leading special projects or initiatives have a similar challenge. They both start with an objective; a plan is then developed and executed to deliver a product, service or result.

To my mind, solving a complex chess position or learning an impossible piece of music is exciting. I like to move from having an idea and at first having no clue how to do it, to the stress and open space of creativity, to building the solution, and then to seeing it come to life and finally delivering an outstanding solution. My mind is always curious, seeking to discover and learn new information. My mind is always creative, looking for innovative ideas and hoping to create something new.

Just as in music, project management also helps bring ideas into reality. It is that power of project management that I like so much. I initially chose my career path for my love of finance. I discovered project management along the way, and it has since fascinated me. Project management is a powerful tool which helps me deliver results and achieve various goals, both in my professional and personal life. It is possible to projectize many areas of our life, as these

---

[1] Wikipedia - Sergei Rachmaninoff
http://en.wikipedia.org/wiki/Sergei_Rachmaninoff
[2] Quote from Sergei Rachmaninoff - Quoteswave.com
http://www.quoteswave.com/text-quotes/46748

concepts are broad and can be applied to many things. A simple example is this book, which is a project on its own.

Learning in life is often a very unusual journey. While becoming an executive and managing a few complex and unusual projects, I also learned the importance of leadership skills. This book integrates my interest in leadership competencies with the world of project management.

Why you should read this book

You have been a project team member, and then a project manager. You now have the opportunity to manage projects of higher complexity. These projects are also more strategically important for your client or organization. You now want to further enhance your skills.

There are numerous books on the various project management tools and techniques, which are very useful and important in your development as a project manager. At this point in your career, you have done your homework and learned the concepts of project management. Yet mastering these concepts only takes you so far. After a certain point, these tools and techniques do not necessarily improve your results or help you address the kind of issues you are facing in your project. You would like to expand your skills further and be able to succeed in managing projects of greater complexity and strategic importance.

You now deal with more senior people in your organization—executives and even members of the C-suite, the top level of the organization. The expectations, availability, communication, and thinking of these senior executives are different. The project environment is also much different. What worked well in simpler projects may no longer be the best approach.

Now you are managing projects in a more dynamic and unpredictable environment. These projects seem to go beyond the basic model of planning the details, executing the tasks, and successfully delivering the result. Something is missing in your skillset. It is time to look beyond planning and monitoring tasks. It is time to focus on leadership skills and add them to your toolbox.

This book was designed with a focus on leadership in project management. By leadership, we mean more than just motivating your team. Leadership includes self-awareness, vision, strategic thinking, decision-making, horizontal integration, stakeholder management, and, of course, team management. It includes people skills applied in various contexts to successfully support the strategy and vision of the project.

This book does not intend to replace or contradict the standard project management tools and techniques. I strongly recommend to all project managers, and anyone working on projects, to master the standard project management concepts. It is a must for your success. I also encourage you to obtain formal education in project management. It is now much easier to do so with the many project management programs available online. Obtaining a professional certification in project management is a strong asset to have.

This book is an expansion of those tools. It is designed to complement your knowledge of project management and help you achieve success at the next level. The objective of this book is to inspire project managers to elevate their thinking and be strategic leaders while managing their projects. The ultimate goal is to achieve better results in a dynamic world.

Contents

CHAPTER 1

The path to project management

From finance to project management

The dream of being a project manager rarely appears at a young age. Yes, it is possible to specifically choose project management as a career, but usually this decision comes later in life. In reality, a university or college student will rarely decide, *"I want to become a project manager."* It is more likely that he will decide to become a scientist, an engineer, a musician, a businessman, and only later will he discover the world of project management. Project management was not my first dream job, either. Like many, I became an accidental project manager.

I remember being a university student and meeting a man who was a retired police officer. He was studying project management to support his second career. Being in my early 20s, I found the project management program at the university odd. I could understand why someone would study accounting, marketing, economics, music, law or whatever else inspired him. But what do you do with a diploma in project management?

My first love was finance. (Well, that's not quite true… My first love was music, even before the first girl I loved, but that is another story. So for the purposes of this book, we'll say that my first love was finance.) I worked for various financial institutions in the 90s and then decided to obtain my accounting designation. I decided to complete the Certified General Accountant (CGA) program in Canada. Later, the three accounting designations in Canada merged, and I am now a CPA, CGA.

I then started to work on various business and audit projects and was exposed to the world of project management. I participated in various projects and then began to manage projects, even special initiatives and emergency projects. I found project management very interesting. Moving from nothing to successfully delivering a specific result is like composing music—It is a fascinating journey.

Like the most sincere friendship, my interest for project management just kept growing and growing. I started to use project management techniques more and more, and even applied them to projects in my personal life. I saw projects everywhere: from business projects to learning programs to family vacations. People close to me heard me talk about project management frequently.

In July 2012, I started Project-Aria, my website dedicated to project management. The website is now a good portion of my life. I interact with others on the topic of project management in various communities and groups on the web, and sometimes in person. The subject has become, more and more, a major part of my life.

Dad, what is project management?

What happens if you often talk about project management? It leads to the famous question: *"What is project management?"* The profession is fascinating for many reasons; one of them is that its concepts can be used for any kind of activity, as long as you have a specific result you are trying to achieve. Project management is so broad, in fact, that it can be hard to understand or explain. Of course, a project manager can quote the *Project Management Body of Knowledge* (PMBOK) definition. You hear it frequently on various podcasts on project management. I simply mean it is hard to explain to those not working in project management.

If you have kids, they will often ask questions about your job. It can be both easy and difficult to explain project management to them, which can lead to some interesting conversations.

Kid: Tell me, Dad, what do you do at work?

Dad: I manage projects.

Kid: Great. What is a project?

Dad: Someone has an idea, and I help them achieve it.

Kid: What kind of idea?

Dad: Well… let me give you an example. I helped my client prepare an office move to a new building.

Kid: Ah! So you work in construction?

And then there is my father. He has also asked me, *"What is project management?"* He hopes that I can give him a clear, concise and eloquent answer. As a former journalist, he hopes that I can bring out of my imagination a lead that will captivate him.

Of course, I can just give him the pure and simple, theoretically correct answer, the textbook definition. After all, my father is an intelligent man. But this will once more lead to the same question:

Dad: *"Okay, I understand… Can you tell me what kind of projects you are doing?"*

It is hard to explain project management without bringing up an example. But once the example is given, the conversation flips to the topic of that example.

This difficulty leads me to ask my own questions: Am I a CPA or PMP? Or am I both? (And that's if we don't bother with the other certifications that I hold.)

Becoming a project manager

I am not alone in facing this identity dilemma. Many project managers have learned the skill of project management second and are first experts in another field. Perhaps one had been working in construction, another is a professional accountant, another is a software programmer, and still another is a graphic designer, a photographer, or a musician. It is often just a secondary evolution of their career that made them project managers. Quite frequently, this is a side effect of success: You have some successes, and you inherit a promotion to the role of project manager. Somehow, your technical expertise is sufficient to be awarded this title.

Often, between fellow project managers, we like to say that we are *Accidental Project Managers*. This expression is so popular that an Internet search will provide many links with this phrase. We became project managers because we were asked at some point to manage a project. Because of our proven technical experience, someone else decided that we could become... a manager. It is a bit of a weak correlation, based on a stretch of the imagination. A person will not necessarily succeed as a manager because he has an in-depth understanding of accounting or is a wizard in spreadsheet programming, graphic design, or software programming.

Alternatively, one may decide to start his own business and sell his services. For some, working on their own is the ultimate career. As an example, a photographer may prefer to start a business to focus his energies on the kind of projects that he really enjoys and excels at doing. With an entrepreneurial spirit, or sometimes a push from destiny like a corporate reorganization, that person starts his business. But in that business, there will be more work than just doing photography. Managing the various projects involved will be equally important.

Either way, you now celebrate your new role and try your best to succeed as a project manager. After all, you are an expert in your specific field, and you deserve this promotion as a recognition of your effort. Your field is a subject that you have mastered and have studied and practiced for a long time. It is your passion, your profession. Surely you will be able to manage this.

Without knowing it, you initiate your journey on the path to becoming not just an expert, but also a manager. You are on a journey to discover the world of project management. This is a world that can bring you to numerous fantastic discoveries for a whole lifetime, but it also comes with a few issues and unexpected challenges.

The burden of the new role

Understanding the role of a manager is the first bridge to cross, as it is not just the title of a position. This often requires a new project manager to face the burden of the responsibilities of the new role. Reality will hit at some point—you can only go so far with technical skills. You have to think of and manage other considerations than just those relating to your expertise in order to be successful. Do you like to code as a programmer? That's fine, but the project will require you to take care of more than just coding to be successful. You will have to consider many new dimensions: budget, communication, procurement, human resources management, and debriefing other intelligent persons who all have an opinion of their own.

You are now in charge. You can no longer rely on someone else to hand you decisions and instructions, and complaining that the orders are not clear is no longer an option. You are the project manager. And if you are working for your own business, the pressure is even more powerful. You have the client as a demanding boss, and your spouse and kids waiting for you to provide an income for the family. Even worse, as the owner of a small new company, you do not have access to all the resources and other experienced employees available in a larger organization. Typically, in the early phase of a business, the team is very small and you are the expert responsible for everything.

The technical details of the scope of the project are already a challenge of their own. But now that you are a project manager, it doesn't stop there. In business language, effectiveness is achieving the objective, and this is, of course, important. Spending a lot of time not achieving any results, or not achieving the intended result, is obviously not a great idea. There are much better uses of your time and resources. But as a project manager, you have clients to please, and effectiveness is not sufficient. You also have to be efficient, which means achieving the objective with the least amount of resources. Resources can include anything: money, of course; materials; time; knowledge and expertise; and so on. In real life, you almost always live with constraints on resources. Your client will also most likely have limited resources and time. Money is limited, deadlines exist, and you can only buy so many materials, skills, assets, or expertise. In addition, in a dynamic, changing world, it is equally important to achieve the result as fast as possible. Otherwise, either competition will beat you to the finish line or the environment will have changed so much that your result will be obsolete.

This initial pressure to learn project management concepts leads to the typical symptoms: long hours at work, unsatisfied clients, frustrated team members, bank account problems, not seeing your kids, and no date night with your spouse. All of these symptoms exist because you have to work long hours during workdays and, even worse, over the weekend to complete this project.

This new role in your career was supposed to be fun and exciting.

There must be another way, you think. Yes! There must be another way.

Many accidental project managers will first try working only with their technical expertise for a few projects. They think, *"Managing can't be so hard, and I'm smart, so I'll just rely on my intelligence, judgment and intuition."* A few scars later, a different kind of wisdom appears with this thought: *"Maybe there is a better way to manage this…."* This is the moment, often after some more pain, that one remembers a piece of advice from an older, more experienced colleague, or a post read somewhere on the Internet, strongly advocating the benefits of project management.

It is interesting to see how a few professional scars can start to make one search for an answer. Hopefully none of these scars have inflicted fatal and permanent wounds in your professional reputation. While making errors is part of life and learning, it is still a good idea to stay away from the fatal ones.

Despite all efforts to do your best and provide an excellent service, your attempts remain insufficient. You need more tools and techniques, an approach to being organized and delivering the expected results with minimum stress and maximum reliability. It is in this context that the discipline of project management becomes very helpful. It gives you an approach developed through many decades, which has a large body of knowledge and numerous publications. With the help of the Internet, you can quickly access tools, forums, and even formal online training and programs to obtain one of the certifications in project management.

At that point, project management stops being a vague concept. It is now a defined methodology. Your toolbox to manage your projects is now expanded. You start to learn, implement, and benefit from the discipline of project management.

CHAPTER 2

Leadership in project management

The discipline of project management

Project management is a fascinating discipline. It is designed to help us achieve a specific result, to help us move from A to B. All organizations have some kind of projects; some organizations are even fully project-based. To state things simply, any result that can be defined and has a beginning and an end can be a project. This definition of project management doesn't delineate the result and can be applied to many different subjects.

You can find various methodologies: As I am a *Project Management Professional* (PMP), my main approach is based on PMBOK, the *Project Management Body of Knowledge* published by the *Project Management Institute* (PMI). Other approaches exist, such as *Prince2*. In the end, they cover the same concepts from different angles, with the same objective of supporting the successful completion of the project. I like Agile methodology for the flexibility it brings to project managers working in a dynamic world.

The current project management theory was first defined in the 20th century, when organizations were based on the operational model with only a few projects. That model was appropriate in the 20th century when the social, business, technological, and cultural environment was still essentially stable. However, this model reads too often as if you can spend two years analyzing something and three years implementing, and then close the project by transferring it to the operations which will do the same thing over and over for the next twenty years.

The context is much different today. By the time you are done analyzing, and even more so by the time you are done implementing, the world will likely have changed. Our world is constantly changing, with an ever-increasing rate of discovery and new knowledge leading to changes. This is a challenge for large organizations with a rigid structure and slow governance structure, both in the public and private sectors. This new environment leads to a much different way to manage business. We now have many organizations that can projectize all their activities.

Let's look at the formal definition of a project in PMBOK:

> "A project is a temporary endeavour undertaken to create a unique product, service, or result. The temporary nature of a project indicates that a project has a definite beginning and end.[3]"

Of course, temporary does not mean that the project duration has to be short—think of a large construction project that spans many years. The key is to be able to identify a defined result, a beginning, and an end. In that sense, project management is rewarding for the achievers, as it is very result-oriented. If you like to see results, project management is for you. You can never be satisfied with the routine or just *"working hard;"* the ultimate celebration is the completion of the unique product, service, or result.

---

[3] Definition of project, PMBOK, 5th edition, p. 3

Some projects are initiated to implement a specific result, some are created to produce small changes, innovation, or transformational initiatives. As long as you have a result, a start, and an end, you have a project. A conference organizer may hold numerous conferences, each of them being a unique project with a start and an end. Building a house is a project, organizing a wedding is a project, and organizing a family vacation is a project.

Project management gives a framework to effectively and efficiently manage what has to be done. It divides the project into five processes: initiating, planning, executing, monitoring and controlling, and closing. It ensures that the project manager thinks holistically about the project and is proactive in the management of the project by giving appropriate attention to the various knowledge areas:

- Project Integration Management
- Project Scope Management
- Project Time Management
- Project Cost Management
- Project Quality Management
- Project Human Resource Management
- Project Communications Management
- Project Risk Management
- Project Procurement Management
- Project Stakeholder Management

The implementation of project management methodology provides benefits such as a higher rate of success, reduction of stress, efficiency in execution, and fewer reactive and more proactive actions thanks to planning and integration of tasks and work packages.

As someone who is learning project management, your life now becomes a mix of technical expertise and project management expertise. You used to be an expert in one field, and now you are also an expert in project management. Ultimately, this method gives you the reputation of achiever, of someone who can deliver what he is asked to. This builds trust with your clients, project sponsors, and project team members.

At this point in your career, you think that project management is a fantastic discovery. If only this discovery had happened earlier in your life.

From project management to leadership

I strongly value learning the details of the tools and techniques used for each of the knowledge areas in project management. A good project manager must have the proper level of mastery of the tools and techniques of project management. This is part of the foundation for project leadership. Through formal training, books, and experience, you should be able to fully understand project management, which is a fundamental element of the value we bring as project manager to our clients. You can find numerous books that will define everything that is involved within each knowledge area. I assume in this book that you have experience in project management and have learned how to manage projects.

Despite this knowledge, you will still face challenges and difficulties in your project. On many occasions, the issue will be deficiencies in the tools and techniques. If the problem relates to an element of the methodology, such as planning, then the solution should revolve around better planning. However, the problem is not always planning, or communication, or scope management, or team management. It is important to assess the root cause of a problem and fix it. You can find experts with a wealth of knowledge and experience to help solve each of them.

However, just as for any other specialty, you can only go so far with technical expertise. For example, an expert in finance needs to develop leadership skills and strategic thinking to perform successfully at a senior level in an organization.

The danger is to think that all issues relate to tools and techniques, which is a dangerous oversimplification of the problem. This view states that if you fully and correctly implement all the processes, you will have a successful project. It is almost as simple as that, according to some books and consultants. Depending on their specialty, these experts will often focus on a specific aspect. Some experts will focus more on planning: just do more planning, and the project will be a success. Another expert may focus on human resource management: use more motivation skills and learn how to delegate, and the project will be a success. Or another expert may focus on communication or on stakeholder management (which are somewhat connected): communicate, and this will solve all problems.

Sometimes a project will face trouble and difficult times because of its leadership. Note that I say sometimes, not always. I don't want to simplify the issue and pretend that leadership is a magic pill. As always, we have to identify the root cause of the problem. Sometimes the problem is project management methodology, and sometimes it is leadership. A proper balance between leadership and project management skills is essential. As project management is used to manage more and more important things in an organization, this means that the whole profession must become a strategic player at the senior executive level. Just as at the senior level in HR, Finance, IT, or Production it is not sufficient to master the various tools and techniques, leadership thus also becomes a key competency required for project success at the senior level.

What is leadership?

It is interesting to see discussions on project leadership appearing more frequently. Leadership skills are an important part of any career development, and this also applies to project management. As one is assigned more complex, strategic projects, he will need to add leadership skills to his toolbox. Leadership skills will be required to understand the why of a project, understand senior management, and ensure the project adds value. A very simple project may only require a focus on task management: planning, assigning, executing, and monitoring progress. However, it doesn't take much to add sufficient complexity to a project to make this approach insufficient. Increased complexity and a dynamic environment will require more than task management from the project manager. This is when leadership skills become essential.

The introduction of leadership skills in project management is an important step in the career of a project manager. Unfortunately, too often discussions about leadership skills narrow the definition of leadership to motivating team members. Project leadership is more than team and task management. Yes, it is better to be a leader than just a boss. A leader will inspire the team and get the best out of them. A good manager is not necessarily a leader. But a leader should also be a good manager to be effective.

You definitely need to be able to manage your activities, and that includes successfully performing the required activities of a manager. Using leadership skills in project management is a complementary approach, not a mutually exclusive approach. Management and leadership should be used together, just as technical competencies work in combination with project management.

The initial journey to becoming a project manager is mostly focused on learning to manage tasks. Unfortunately, the consequence is that too often project managers limit their role to task supervisors. I like to call this level being a taskmaster. It is as if the only role of the project manager were to create a plan for tasks, delegate tasks, execute the tasks in the plan, and deliver the result. I want project managers to go beyond the role of taskmaster, to rise to the level of project leaders, with the ability to have a vision, strategic thinking, and decision-making to achieve success in their project.

The dimensions of leadership

Project management is a very powerful approach to achieving results. However, to get the most out of it, it is important to go beyond task delivery and raise our approach to the level of leadership. In this book, I would like to explore how leadership can benefit project managers and help them achieve better results in their projects, especially in a dynamic world which requires rapid changes and the aptitude for swift and effective decision-making.

In this book, we will focus on leadership skills and the ability to make decisions. Project managers will enhance their careers by developing these competencies. To have a holistic view of leadership, we will start first with the foundation of leadership and a look at the leader as a person. Too often this is absent from project management books, or possibly the last chapter, but I think it should come first in the discussion. Without the view of the leader as a person, leadership skills are on weak ground. Without considering the leader as a person, we would have a very limited tool to develop leadership skills in a profound and sustainable manner.

Leadership is the ability to create and communicate a vision, develop a strategy, and lead that strategy through all phases to achieve an objective. Leadership requires the ability to think strategically, make decisions, and interact with others. In a dynamic world full of constant and quick changes, leadership is a critical skill.

Good leadership must be built and developed on a strong foundation. Often, books on leadership will go directly to actions that a leader should take to lead a team. This is like an organization that focuses wholly on actions, without thinking about its vision, culture, values and ethics, and governance. This is why we will focus first on the foundation and the leader as a person.

Leadership will be discussed in the next chapters, covering the following topics:

Chapter 3: requirements for a solid foundation to be a good project manager.

Chapter 4: the leader as a person and important considerations for being a successful leader.

Chapter 5: values and ethics, an important element in managing teams, relationships, and decision-making.

Chapter 6: the importance of people in project management.

Chapter 7: team leadership and the application of leadership skills to managing your projects and project team.

Chapter 8: effective delegation in the context of the project.

Chapter 9: strategic thinking to optimize project success.

Chapter 10: the power of reality and the importance of facing it with honesty.

Chapter 11: the biggest challenges of project managers.

Chapter 12: keys to project success.

Chapter 13: a strategic view of planning.

Chapter 14: managing the project with a leadership view.

Chapter 15: project reports to support strategic leadership.

Chapter 16: decision-making for effective leadership.

We have to be more than experts to succeed in managing projects. We need leadership. This is what this book is trying to do: bring leadership to project management and help you achieve better results.

For project managers who have experience with and substantial knowledge of project management, this book should help you achieve more results by combining project management with leadership skills. In the end, the goal is to achieve better results in a dynamic world.

CHAPTER 3

The foundation

Introduction

This book deals primarily with leadership and decision-making. The objective of the book is to help project managers develop leadership skills and achieve better results. If a project manager is interested in managing more complex projects with strategic importance for the organization, he will have to develop leadership skills. You can achieve only so much just with technical expertise.

Does this mean that leadership alone can make someone a good project manager? Let's be clear on this: The answer is absolutely not! In a holistic model, you need all parts of the model to achieve optimal success. Although this book focuses on leadership, it does assume that project managers have established a strong foundation underneath. Leadership alone may give you an intense feeling of being an imposter. It is important to establish a strong foundation first before focusing on leadership skills.

This foundation includes four parts:

- Technical knowledge
- Project management knowledge
- Experience
- Continuous learning

Even though this book is focused on leadership, you cannot have leadership without this solid foundation. That is why we must start with a quick review. This chapter explores each of the four parts of the foundation.

Technical knowledge

Project management is an approach that can be used to manage any kind of project. This can include the development of a new product, a research paper, composing a music album, a space exploration project, a wedding, a conference, a bridge construction, or a business acquisition. All of these are similar because they are projects; all of them are different because they relate to different skills. For some, you need to be an engineer; for others, a musician, a scientist, an event organizer, or an accountant.

Successfully managing a project requires two kinds of knowledge: project management knowledge and technical knowledge. Most often, project managers learn their technical expertise first and then later add the needed project management expertise to their resume.

Sometimes we hear debates as to which kinds of expertise a project manager should have. Does the project manager need to have specific knowledge related to the subject of the project? Or can he successfully manage any kind of project? It should be noted that this is usually a discussion only between project managers. We rarely hear a project sponsor saying that he just wants a project manager with no understanding of the subject.

As a CPA, CGA in Canada, most of my projects are related to business processes, accounting, and auditing. This is my expertise. I am not the right person to manage the construction of a bridge or a plane. Honestly, I recommend that you do not cross the bridge if I was the person managing the construction.

Sometimes you will hear the example of how a music conductor relates to the role of a project manager. It is used to show that you can lead a group without playing each instrument. As a musician, I choke when I hear this example given as proof that you can be a project manager without the technical expertise related to the project. A musical conductor is absolutely an expert in music. That he is not a flute soloist is irrelevant. The conductor knows far more about music and the flute, and all other instruments, than most could care to learn in their lifetime. Is he necessarily a virtuoso on all instruments? No, and he doesn't have to be. But he definitely possesses a deep knowledge of music and of each instrument so he can have a meaningful conversation and provide coherent and logical instructions to the musicians.

Having sufficient knowledge of the subject is critical. You do not need to be an expert in all the activities, but you do need to have a clear understanding of what is required in the project. Otherwise, you have a huge, self-inflicted project management risk: the risk that you do not have the appropriate knowledge to manage the project.

At the beginning of a project, you must assess your knowledge in the subject and the depth of your knowledge gap. The bigger the gap, the more project management risks and blind spots you will be facing.

If the risk is big, it is essential to be honest and understand that the project will require adding research to the planning phase. A potential strategy is to have a second in command who has the technical knowledge of the project's subject. Adding appropriate subject matter experts is also a good approach. To some, this approach shows that you can be a project manager without knowing the technical side of the project. I think it actually proves that it is essential to know the technical side as a project manager. It is so essential that if you don't have the knowledge, you must take appropriate measures to compensate. And there is a risk and a cost to that.

It may be nice theoretically to say that a good project manager can manage any project. In reality, even if it were true, we cannot ignore the cost of the solution, which would have to be pushed as an additional and unnecessary cost to the client. From a lean approach and value added perspective, why would a client want to pay more because the proposed or selected project manager can only provide project management knowledge?

It is fundamentally important to know your area of expertise. It is part of the foundation required to adequately manage projects. It is your professional obligation to accept projects that you have sufficient expertise to manage successfully. Don't pretend! (Do you hear the song *"The Great Pretender"* by The Platters?[4]) You do not need to be the ultimate expert in everything. You must understand the subject to the level of being able to engage in intelligent conversations on it with the project sponsor, team members, and stakeholders.

You need to know your expertise—what kind of projects are your core expertise, and what projects are related to your expertise. You should not try to manage something completely unrelated to your strengths. That would only be playing to your weaknesses.

Project management knowledge

This book complements project management knowledge; it does not supersede it. As part of the foundation of being a project leader, you must have a strong knowledge in project management. There is no shortcut. Solid project management knowledge is important. All the good will and great leadership skills in the world will not get the project

---

[4] Wikipedia - The Great Pretender
http://en.wikipedia.org/wiki/The_Great_Pretender

done if you lack expertise in the subject area and the core principles of project management. Even if a result can be accomplished, it will not be completed with the best use of time and resources.

There is a rich body of knowledge available on project management. It starts with the Project Management Body of Knowledge, published by the Project Management Institute. Numerous books cover the various techniques on project management. You can find books specialized in each knowledge area in project management: for instance, project planning, contract management, the work breakdown structure, human resource management, risk management, and financial management.

Obtaining the proper knowledge is vital for success. As I mentioned earlier, project management is often a secondary knowledge, and people become project managers by accident. It may feel like you can manage projects on your own, using just your judgment, experience, and management skills. You may have the privilege of managing more complex and strategic projects and feel that your focus should go directly to leadership. Again, the answer is absolutely no. You have to first establish a solid foundation.

As project managers, let's ensure that we bring the most value to our clients. One may be able to deliver results in an informal way, without using project management techniques. But that path will always be inefficient at best. Project management techniques will enhance quality and success, and reduce issues and problems during the life of the project. Frustrations will be reduced, and trust from the project sponsor, clients, and other key stakeholders will be increased.

Acquiring the knowledge to be a good project manager is done in four parts. The first is work experience. We must have some practical experience, not just an intellectual knowledge of project management.

The second part is learning. Knowledge can be acquired through various options, including books, seminars, websites, PMI local chapters, forums, Google+ communities, and LinkedIn groups.

The third level is formal education. There are numerous benefits that can only be obtained through completing formal courses. Despite all attempts to be dedicated in self-learning, there is still a form of discipline that exists in formal courses that cannot be replaced. At a minimum, it is useful to have a comprehensive introductory course on project management. This can be done the old-fashioned way, physically in a college or university, but technology has opened the door to a new, more flexible option: online courses. Because I work full time and have a spouse and two sons, I enjoy a lot taking online courses from universities rather than attending physically. After your introductory course, it is your choice if you want to complete a full program or just go directly to the fourth and last level, the professional certification.

Certification is definitely something those working in project management should seek. It is a good way to acquire knowledge, show professionalism, and build trust when dealing with senior management and stakeholders.

Experience

Project management is the art of bringing ideas to reality. A good project manager is someone who can deliver results. As much as theory, methodology, and planning can be interesting, success is still measured by delivering the intended product, service, or results.

The third part of the foundation is experience. There are two types of experience. The first one is the technical experience with the subject of the project, and the second is the experience in managing projects of similar complexity.

An experienced project manager can provide a lot of value and help the project succeed. An experienced project manager can come in, quickly assess what needs to be done, make a decision (or a recommendation) on the proposed plan and methodology, and successfully deliver results. There is no *"one size fits all"* in project management. This is where experience can help.

It is the usual view that an experienced project manager should cost more, but it is important to keep in mind that this higher cost is not meant to be a reward for that experience. This justification for a higher price is selfish and not the best approach to meet the needs of the client. Clients pay a higher price to acquire the efficiency gains that experience can bring. These gains should be sufficient to more than offset the higher cost. If the experience is relevant to the project and is still current, then it will result in achieving higher quality at a lower cost.

As long as the experience is rich, diverse, and recent, it can help. One can have twenty years of experience and repeat the same knowledge for over twenty years, with no new learning or improvements. In such cases, the lack of knowledge and experience in newer concepts, tools, and techniques will be a liability for the project.

And this brings us to the last part of the foundation: continuous learning.

Continuous learning

We now live in a very dynamic world, with a fast pace of innovation and changes. It is important to understand that knowledge itself is also dynamic. Not too long ago in the history of humanity, the pace of innovation was slow enough that you could study something and apply it in the same way for the rest of your life. An apprentice learning a skill such as masonry or baking would learn exactly the same skills and knowledge as his master had learned. A son would learn exactly the same skills as his father had learned twenty years ago. Training and education would pass almost the same skills and knowledge from one generation to the next. At best, one might see one significant change in his lifetime.

We now face a paradigm shift. Acquiring a specific technical knowledge and project management knowledge, including maintaining your certification, and then relying only on experience is no longer appropriate. With the pace of innovation, this approach is now obsolete and even dangerous. We may end up with experience and knowledge in our resume, but with both of them becoming obsolete more than we want to admit, and faster than we can imagine.

Continuous learning is fundamental for the career of a project manager. Learning in the modern world is no longer a phase of life in your early 20s. It has to be a continuous activity, a lifestyle. You should make it a personal value to constantly learn and maintain your professional knowledge. Learn continuously and avoid making the same mistakes repetitively. Watch people you admire, and learn when you can from the mistakes of others. You have to seek any opportunities to expand your ideas, rather than crystalize them and repeat the same concepts for thirty or forty years.

As a matter of fact, the PMP certification requires those with the certification to complete Professional Development Units (PDUs) during a period of three years to maintain their certification. For success, this requirement should be viewed as the minimum, not as a target. There are various ways to learn: books, audiobooks, project management sites, podcasts, forums, communities, online courses, classes, and seminars.

Continuous learning is also a leadership skill. You will increase your ability to have a vision for your project, create an appropriate strategy, influence people (your team and stakeholders), and make effective decisions with current knowledge during the life of the project.

Because of the constantly changing world in which we live, a leader should be careful about himself. His own experience and knowledge, with time, can be both an asset and a liability, a strength and a weakness. Yes, as a leader you can perform many things with success because of your past experience and knowledge. That is why you have the position and have been hired to do the job. However, there is another side to this. As a leader, you must avoid the trap of repeating the same techniques and concepts for twenty years. Even a great concept will require updates over time. This is how knowledge progresses; it is based on constant evolution.

As Albert Einstein (1879-1955[5]) said:

> "We can't solve problems by using the same kind of thinking we used when we created them.[6]"

Conclusion

A firm foundation is essential for a career in project management. Once it has been established, developing leadership skills is the next step. The next chapter will focus on the leader as a person. This is the first step to ensuring the development of real leadership skills that will have a profound impact on a career. As a matter of fact, most executive development programs will start there. I

[5] Wikipedia - Albert Einstein
http://en.wikipedia.org/wiki/Albert_Einstein
[6] Quote from Albert Einstein - Quoteswave.com
http://www.quoteswave.com/picture-quotes/374058

believe that leadership development for program managers should also start with an honest view of the person. This view covers who we are and what we bring (and should bring) to our projects with our actions, behaviors, emotions, and personality.

CHAPTER 4

The leader

Introduction

To advance your career in project management and increase your successes, you need superior interpersonal skills. Leadership is not a position of solitude; a leader has to interact with others. You are not just working with task lists, Gantt charts, and spreadsheets. You need to be able to work with people—this is non-negotiable. Your work will include many interactions with other people to listen, to communicate, to convince, to obtain their approval, or to share the vision of the project. We will come to that. But let's start by looking at the leader as a person.

Too often, leadership discussions are solely focused on others. It is as if the only reason to care about leadership is so we can improve relationships with others and what we can obtain from them. Too many leadership discussions are focused on how to influence and motivate others—your team members or other stakeholders. It is as if the leader himself doesn't exist or is not part of the equation.

A holistic view of leadership begins with the leader as a person. After all, we are the person we spend the most time with. So the discussion should start with this question: *Can we have enough leadership to influence our own vision, convince ourselves, and get ourselves to achieve our best performance?* We have to start there for real, profound, and sustainable leadership. The leader is a human being, not a robot, so let's view him as a person and not confuse him with a piece of artificial intelligence from a science-fiction movie which makes decisions based solely on mathematical models.

This chapter will review essential elements of the leader as a person that influence his professional performance. For effective leadership, it is important to integrate with our behavior the key qualities of a leader and to develop a high level of self-awareness. You cannot have high emotional and social intelligence with others and a weak awareness of your own self and emotions. It is also important to maintain a healthy lifestyle. We are just one person, with one body and one mind. Strategic project management requires top performance, and top performance requires having a holistic view of the leader as a person, including health.

Qualities of a leader

Agility

A leader needs to have the ability to change, be nimble, and continuously improve. Agility is powerful. It lets an organization and a project team be flexible and make a quick analysis of a rapidly changing environment, a dynamic environment, or a more complete set of information. With agility, it is possible to make decisions and adapt quickly.

Being agile changes our perception of many things. Protecting the ego of our past decisions is no longer an issue. We can easily admit that the previous decision was or is no longer the best, and protect the success of the project by making a new decision based on the most current information. Children naturally have this ability to be agile and flexible. They have no previous learning or ego to protect and are just eager to learn all the time. Sometimes, however, with knowledge, education, and experience, this agility is unfortunately lost.

Agility means that we see our process as tools in our toolbox which we use as needed, depending on the requirements of our project. Agility provides a means to adapt and succeed in a dynamic and changing world.

Curiosity

Project managers must be curious, and always be on a quest to learn and discover new things. As project managers, we are supposed to be change agents. Yet somehow this does not always happen. Sometimes when you read books on project management, you get the feeling that project managers like to always use the same methodology, approach, and tools. Sometimes, it feels like the objective of project management is to impose our discipline on clients. Instead, we should be curious about the various needs of our clients, in order to properly understand and support them. Cultivating curiosity is a strong quality of leadership.

Optimism

The next quality is optimism, which is important for you and for your team. In a project, there will always be difficulties. Sometimes the rationale for the project itself is to solve a problem. So if you feel stressed when facing difficulties and tend to be scared of the unknown, it will not be a good thing. The project team, the sponsor, and the stakeholders will all feel this lack of optimism, and this negativity will have consequences. Teams perform better in a positive environment; stakeholders collaborate better when the project is associated with hope and optimism.

Despite all attempts to plan and control work packages, tasks, milestones, and deliverables, a project will still have unknowns and things that change. You will have to lead and make decisions along the way. You have to be able to see through circumstances and believe that you will succeed.

Communication

Communication is an essential quality for leadership. Many activities of a project manager involve communication, and all humans communicate in their own ways, even if using the same language. Each person comes with his own background, context, and communication style preferences. Some like details, while some prefer overall summaries. A project requires understanding of many complex business requirements and tasks to be completed, yet it is important to be able to identify and simplify the key messages that should be communicated.

A leader benefits from being able to understand the needs of others and communicate strategically. The timing of communication is essential to the success of a leader, just as it is important to use the proper form of communication. Some discussions are better done by email, some in person, and some in a group meeting. Finally, communication also applies to decision-making. The leader will have to communicate his decisions, or communicate with others to obtain key decisions.

Project management includes many interactions with other persons. Communication is everywhere. As such, to be an effective leader, you have to be able to communicate, with a proper balance between listening and providing information.

Continuous improvement

We mentioned the fact that we now live in a very dynamic world, characterized with fast changes and innovations. As such, a leader who doesn't want to continuously learn will soon become a burden to an organization. Knowledge and experience can now become obsolete much faster than most are ready to admit. In a competitive environment, the quality of continuous learning and improvement is essential to maintain an edge over the competition.

The ultimate learning strength is to be able to have an opinion, research it further, change opinions based on new facts and thinking, and accept the new opinion with no shame or regrets. This is how humans evolve and how continually acquire new knowledge. Children can do this very naturally, and this ability should not be lost.

With the speed of change in the social and business environment, technology, and innovations, it is important to keep an agile mind. Maintaining the status quo in our dynamic world is becoming the most dangerous risk in management. Valuing continuous improvement is one of the key qualities of a leader in a dynamic world, and it has to be consciously cultivated as a lifestyle.

Self-Awareness

True leadership development starts with the Self. Before a leader can effectively influence others, he must first focus on himself. If changing your own behavior is beyond your limits, then how can you claim to be able to influence others? Leadership development must start with a focus on the leader as a person.

The first step is self-awareness. You can only influence the impact of your emotions on decisions by being aware of their existence. Good executive leadership development programs include tools to increase self-awareness of strengths, weaknesses, personality, and emotions. These tools enhance our awareness of our own emotions and those of others. This approach should not be limited to executive development, however. It is also applicable in project management.

A leader must be aware of his personal behavior, biases, opinions, cultural preferences, strengths, and weaknesses, as well as his emotions and social behavior. In his leadership role, his emotions (or lack of them) will influence the behavior of others. After all, the leader is not only an intellectual person, having a vision, strategic thinking, and making decisions. He is not a robot in charge of other robots. The leader is a human being, constantly dealing with other human beings. His success will be strongly influenced by his own emotions and thoughts. His influence on others will be determined first by his social behaviors, emotions, and thoughts, long before the intellectual part of his leadership.

With the insights of self-awareness, the first person that the leader will influence is himself. With this awareness, he can influence his feelings, thoughts, and behaviors. It would be weak for a leader only to see faults in others and pretend to be perfect himself. Such leaders are emotionally blind, and this blindness is impacting their perceptions of themselves and others.

In leadership development, it is important to pause periodically and take the time to assess our strengths and weaknesses. There are tools and various personality tests available to help with this, which are useful in identifying our strengths and weaknesses, and in understanding where you are now in your life. They are a snapshot in time, and they can provide significant insight and guide your personal and professional development. However, a word of caution is probably required to obtain the maximum benefits. These tools should be combined with the results of modern research in neuroscience. As an example, neuroplasticity is an interesting concept, proving through various researches that the brain can change and adapt. The brain's plasticity is much greater than many would think. This explains the profound changes that some people can experience during their life. Mixing these two concepts gives us more insight and the flexibility to evolve as needed. Otherwise, a personality test can become the prison of a label.

Ultimately, the leader should understand that their own behavior is the best they can ask of their team. I would even take it one step further: the leader should expect more of himself than of his team. Self-awareness is an essential requirement to be able to influence our own behavior.

Health and nutrition

Very often, projects must be done in high-performance mode, with periods of intense work. It is easy in this mode to focus only on short-term tasks. However, if we forget to take care of ourselves, our success can be very short term. It is a dangerous trap. We all have heard cases of a career stopped by a burnout. Their success was impressive, but more like a burning meteor. It is not wise to think we are immune to that scenario. It does not just happen to others. Just like a machine needs maintenance, your body does also.

This burnout happens a lot in our culture of busyness, where being busy is sometimes the most glorified goal. We almost forget what results we are supposed to achieve and focus on being busy instead. However, working hard can be a very bad indicator of success. One can work hard and not produce much. Productivity should instead be measured by the results achieved. In an infinite quest for top performance, we can develop the habit of working hard, very hard, and even too hard. The ultimate worst scenario is working hard your whole career, not seeing your family and children, and dying a few weeks or months after retirement.

The number of hours that you put in the job shouldn't be the key performance indicator. What should matter are the results that you can achieve. We don't want employees to just be present at work. We want them to be able to produce measurable results.

Health and nutrition are important to achieve top performance as measured by results, not busyness. The world of sports understands this concept. An athlete cannot always be in performance mode, even if he loves his sport. He has to balance performance, training, nutrition, health, and sleep.

Project management is similar to sports. Performance is the ability to work and deliver the project. As project managers, we are not robots, nor is our team. Proper nutrition is important for long-term performance. To achieve the highest level of success, you need to develop a sustainable model.

To optimize productivity and achieve top performance, leaders must be wise enough to understand the importance of taking care of their health. Athletes know that they must integrate nutrition and rest in their schedule to achieve top performance. This balance is just as important for us, as the leader of the project; it is also important for our team members.

Sleep

High performance requires that we maintain healthy habits, which include eating well and sleeping. Unfortunately, sleep is very often the disposable hero of a culture of busyness, in which we measure being busy and not the results we accomplish in a day. We forget that sleeping is an essential component of maintaining good health. Too often, lack of sleep is worn like a badge of honor.

As project managers, we often tend to have very busy and chaotic schedules. We must blitz to reach milestones, live through fast-paced projects, and manage everything else that could possibly happen. We often must work hard for the success of our projects. I know how easy it is to work late, very late, often much too late, and then have shortened nights. Then, the next day, we rely on coffee and sweets to maintain our productivity level. Thus the cycle starts again.

Working long hours in the evening and relying on coffee to save us from the damage of a short night should not be viewed as the best option. It is something we at times have to do; that's a fact. But when it happens, we should be conscious of its impact on our health and our capacity to perform. If we measure results, a rested mind and body is more productive than a tired one.

There is a bit of a glorification of busyness in the profession. The belief is often that someone working long hours must be an excellent worker. But the final judgment on a performance should rest only on results. Long hours are sometimes impossible to avoid, and it would be naive to claim otherwise. However, there is a planning problem if that is the norm. If a team is always fighting fires, maybe someone on the team is an arsonist! Let's hope it is not the project leader!

The ultimate frontier of the busyness approach is to neglect sleep. Some are proud of always working late at night or over the weekend, 60 or 80 hours a week. They will reduce their sleeping hours to the bare minimum and often compensate with coffee. There is the belief that sleep is optional, can be reduced, and is just a waste of time.

But what are the hidden effects of lack of sleep? Recent medical research is producing interesting results on the importance of sleep for optimal health and performance. The more I am aware of this, the more I discover interesting articles on the subject. Sleep is an inherent part of how the human body works—as project managers, we must face this reality. The impact of lack of sleep only stays hidden for a while.

Based on the research, wouldn't it be better to manage our energy, our body, and our mind, and respect sleep and its power? I used to be a big offender on this subject, staying very late to work on all the things I like to do. I must say that I was busier then, but I am now more productive. Strange paradox…

It is important to remember that work tends to expand with the amount of time available. Consequently, it is good to set time boundaries on tasks. Time boundaries force innovation and encourage us to find the most efficient way to do a task. Without boundaries, effort invested in an activity tends to evolve upward significantly.

Sports and fitness used to be only focused on training. Then it changed to focus on training and nutrition. Now we see many training programs that include appropriate consideration for training, nutrition, and sleep. Why? Because the optimization of results depends on a holistic approach aligned with the way the human body works. Sleep, just like nutrition, is a fundamental part of recovery and development. Therefore, for top performance, it should be included in the training program.

It seems athletes are now aware of the importance of rest, recovery, and sleep in achieving top performance. For knowledge workers, sleep will enhance mental performance and enable the person to analyze better and faster. Tasks will take less time to complete because of higher mental clarity and sharpness. Communication and stakeholders' engagement will become better and clearer. Appropriate sleep hours are an important part of performance.

It is nice to see this subject now appearing more often in the world of productivity. Athletes understand the importance of sleep, and leaders and professional workers can also benefit from it. To better achieve your goals, enjoy your pillow and sleep! Let that sleep enhance your career and even your personal life.

Personal Life

As a project manager, you may end up having more and more responsibilities as you get promotions in your career, and it may be tempting to spend all your time at work. After all, there is still work to do. The problem with this logic is that there will always be work to do. Your mind is not a computer—you need to rest.

It is tempting to stay connected all the time, provide responses via smartphone within five minutes, and stay connected during the weekend. It is tempting to bring work to your vacation, at the beach or the mountain resort, which means no real vacation for you. It also sends a message to your team that you don't trust them.

Why do we pretend from time to time that we can separate work and personal life? We are just one person. We don't live a double life, one as a professional person at work, and the second one at home. Some talk about work-life balance, but in the end, it is more a question of achieving a healthy integration of your work and personal life.

It is hard for anyone, you or a member of your team, to achieve top performance if they don't have some balance in their life. It is healthy for productivity to take a vacation. It is good to go back home and enjoy an evening away from the challenges of work. There is an old piece of wisdom that says we should sleep on it—so let your mind rest.

For top performance, it is our responsibility to have a holistic view of life. We must take care of ourselves as a person. This includes self-awareness, personal development, nutrition, physical and mental health, and sleep. It also includes taking care of our personal life.

It is healthy to have hobbies and other interests outside of work. Otherwise, work becomes too consuming. Work is with you, in your mind, everywhere. Problems at work burn all your mental energy by occupying your thoughts 24 hours, seven days a week. With other personal interests, you can give your brain a break, rest, and some peace of mind.

Let yourself have a holistic view of success and of your life. It will not dilute your results. As a matter of fact, you will find that you become even more productive at work.

Mind and stress

Have you ever met a leader who forgets to take care of his mind: thoughts, emotions, and stress? In a high-performance environment, it is easy to think that our mind should focus only on work, like a machine. Often, we can see some people trying to act as if we are computers and can sandbox our mind, isolating the project management part from other parts. However, stress, thoughts, and emotions will have an impact on performance.

A more accurate description of reality is that we are just one person, and everything in us is connected. Because of that, self-awareness and self-care are very important. We must know who we are as a person, with our strengths and weaknesses. It includes being aware of our preferences, the preferences of others, and how the two can interact with each other.

Taking care of one's health starts, of course, with physical health. It begins with eating well to support the body and the mind functioning at their optimal level. You can only function for so long without good food.

Physical exercise is the next step. Your job may provide you with enough physical exercise, or it may be more sedentary. The mind does perform better with a healthy body. There is no hard separation between the two. After all, if the body fails, it has significant consequences on our life. This does not mean you need an intense training program. Sure, you can train for a marathon or a half-marathon, or you can subscribe to a league or a gym, but the solution can start with something very simple. Just make sure your body moves sufficiently during the week.

This also applies when you organize day-long meetings. Schedule breaks and let participants move. You will get more productivity out of the day if you do so. Some teams and organizations even hold standing meetings. First of all, you get more energy out of participants. Second, it forces the meeting to be action-oriented and focused on results, since, while people can *"tolerate"* a long sitting meeting, they get tired faster in a standing meeting.

I remember having a team member who was stressed with the workload. She explained to me that she had to do four different things and didn't know where to start or how it could all be done before the deadlines. Too many milestones were colliding at the same time. What did I do as her manager? It was at the end of the afternoon, and I knew she was about to work late in the evening, just to survive this difficult moment. I told her to go home, rest, forget work, do something else like watch a movie with her spouse and family, have fun with her child, sleep well, and we would talk the next morning.

She was shocked. It was an unusual response from a boss. Yet the next morning, she was calm, arrived earlier, and was able to focus and complete the work required.

In the end, we are not robots with a computer as a brain which can sandbox applications. It is important to take care of yourself as a person and let your employees do the same.

The truth is very simple: we are just one person. It is much easier to perform well at work with a peaceful mind, good health, and rested body. After all, results are what we are trying to achieve in project management. Our legacy as a leader should be our accomplishments, not the tired bodies we left behind.

How do you de-stress?

Stress in some ways is unavoidable in project management. It is part of working, and I would say it is even more prominent today when you are working as a project manager. We manage initiatives that are less predictable than a repetitive operational environment. While we don't control the environment and what is happening, we can manage our own reactions. When stress happens, what do we do to de-stress?

This is an important chapter for leadership. If you don't learn to manage your stress, it will reduce your productivity. Even more importantly, it will reduce your leadership ability. Not only will you be less able to lead a team, motivate them, and obtain their best contributions, but even worse, stress will weaken your ability to make quick and sound decisions. Ultimately, it will impact our performance at work and can lead to bad managerial practices. Over the long term, excessive stress can lead to burnout or long-term physical damage to the body, such as cardiovascular problems.

In addition, if we are stressed, we are sending stress signals to the whole team and the stakeholders. This generates a negative impact on the performance of the whole team. There is a huge difference between being action-oriented in an urgent context and fostering panic among the group. Broadcasting stress to everyone will foster panic and impact the sustainability and cohesion of the team. Some team members may leave for a better work environment;

others may refuse to join because of the stressful reputation of the project.

So it is important to establish in our life as a leader a mechanism to deal effectively with stress. This starts, of course, with self-awareness, being able to recognize stress in ourselves. Various methods can be used to de-stress. Among others, we should list first refusing to glorify busyness, focusing on results, and keeping the real nature of your project in perspective.

It is then a matter of taking care of ourselves as human beings: meditation, sports, and nutrition. Do not forget your family in the process. Nobody has ever said on their death bed, *"I wish I had seen less of the significant people in my life and more of my work."*

Having other activities and interests in your life balances the mind and keeps you from obsessing all day long over work. Anything can do: photography, music, painting, dancing, or cooking. Just pick something you enjoy. It's your choice, but you must have a mechanism to de-stress.

Conclusion

In the end, if you don't take care of yourself, nobody will. If you want to optimize performance, just like top athletes, you need a holistic view of yourself. Leadership positions can be very rewarding, but they can also be very short-term if you ignore the human side of the leader. A person who ignores mental, physical, emotional, and psychological well-being is destined to fail.

This chapter should not be an afterthought, positioned as the last chapter of a book. It is not something to consider later in life when you have the time. Top athletes have comprehensive programs, including performance, training, nutrition, sleep, and emotions. This helps them achieve their best performance even in the most stressful competitions. Top leaders should follow the same principles. To achieve the best level of leadership in project management, the same holistic approach is vital.

CHAPTER 5

Values and ethics

Introduction

A leader will have to make decisions on the intended results, strategies, proposed action plan, response to issues, seizing opportunities, and reacting to challenges from the environment. He will also react to many issues, events, and behaviors of others. These leadership actions and decisions are never purely intellectual. They are influenced by other factors, including our values and ethics. Of course, good judgment is required first and foremost for proper leadership, but without values and ethics, good judgment can be insufficient.

When facing a decision, a challenge, or any situation, how does the project manager handle it? Project leaders interact at more than one level with many different types of people who have different cultural backgrounds, sometimes in many different countries. Leaders are faced with ethical dilemmas throughout their careers, and the right answer may be different depending on your organization and culture. The most important thing is to be able to have a dialog on the topic.

Values and ethics are behaviors as well as fundamental choices that define who we are. They influence our thoughts, behaviors, and decisions. Values and ethics are neither a form nor an annual event. Various forms may document our awareness of a code of ethics or of any potential conflict of interests and can support this process within an organization, and the process can be enhanced by annual events where the subject is discussed. However, one should never assume that he has completed his annual contribution to values and ethics because he has completed the mandatory forms and participated in the prescribed events.

Values and ethics are a human behavior and a leadership skill. They are more than just an event or a compliance requirement. They are necessary for strong leadership, to build trust and achieve success in project management. Tone at the top is important, as any management control framework will note. Recent history has, unfortunately, shown us examples of the catastrophic consequences of a lack of ethics at the top in some large organizations.

What are your values, and what are those of your organization? Are values discussed in your organization? Or is it just a subject to be politely ignored? If it is discussed, is it a one-day event or a common social behavior? As a leader, you should be aware of the organizational and cultural environment in which your project operates. You should not rely solely on formal initiatives in an organization, but should also periodically include a discussion with your team on values and ethics. Even more importantly, your team members should feel comfortable discussing values and ethics during the life of your project.

Values and ethics are key components of the governance structure of an organization. This also applies to project management. PMI has a Code of Ethics and Professional Conduct which all PMI members and credential holders must sign, agreeing to adhere to a high standard of ethical behavior. It is important for project managers to know the code, which means more than reading it before passing the PMP exam to obtain your certification.

This starts with us as a person. Our behavior must demonstrate strong values and ethics. As a leader, you cannot claim to support certain values and ethics and then behave differently. It would be inappropriate to use them as a code to impose on others without first focusing on our own behavior. First and foremost, we must express our values and ethics in our daily behavior. A leader cannot expect more of others than he expects from himself.

A leader must set the example. He should demonstrate strong values and ethics to his team members and stakeholders by his behavior and his decisions. Team members will observe the behavior at the top and reach their own conclusions about ethics based on their observations, not on speeches and official organizational documents. Because of this, leaders must set high standards for themselves.

It is important to give enough space in your leadership and governance structure to values and ethics. There is a difference between discussing the topic in theory and dealing with real problems with a proper consideration of values and ethics. The first part is important to have and should not be overlooked, but the second one is the real challenge, and it will require courage.

Many professional organizations have set a code of conduct or code of ethics, and those who have acquired certifications from different professional organizations often have different codes to adhere to, sometimes in addition to the code of the organization they work for. It can seem complicated, but at least all these codes are mostly centered on the same concepts and ideas. They can be summarized in a few words by the old principles of doing the right things, being fair, and being able to be transparent. If you have to do a secret deal or hide something, you are probably on the wrong path.

Let's use the *PMI Code of Ethics and Professional Conduct*, which describe expectations, ideals, and mandatory behaviors, to do an overview of the subject. The purpose of this Code is to instill confidence in the project management profession and to help an individual become a better practitioner. This Code will assist us in making wise decisions, particularly when faced with difficult situations where we may be asked to compromise our integrity and values.

The PMI code affirms four values: responsibility, respect, fairness, and honesty. Let's do an overview of these four values and how they relate to leadership in project management.

Responsibility

Responsibility is our ownership for the decisions we make or fail to make, the actions we take or fail to take, and the consequences that result. In addition, a leader should be happy to let the team shine for successes and protect them in case of a problem. It is bad leadership to take the honor of all successes and *"throw the team under the bus"*, as we say, for all failures. It is also bad leadership to consider your project team to be perfect and blame all issues on other units in the organization or on external stakeholders.

Our chapter on the foundation stressed the importance of technical knowledge, project management knowledge, and experience. These three dimensions complement one another. Project managers should accept only those assignments that are consistent with their background, experience, skills, and qualifications. Others hire us to deliver results, and we should commit to managing a project only if we honestly know we can manage it and add value in the process.

Courage is essential in leadership. It is important as a leader not to hide issues, errors, or omissions. We must have the courage to communicate the issue or problem in a timely manner and be solution-oriented. It is impossible to be solution-oriented if we hide facts under stones. We must create a culture in which it is possible for others, including our team members, to communicate negative information.

A key requirement for ethical decisions is to be fully aware of the legal and cultural environment and not rush to a conclusion without having all the facts. Not being judgmental and taking the time to gather and analyze the facts is important. We should not accuse others of ethical misconduct too quickly unless we have all the facts.

Respect

Respect is our duty to show a high degree of honor and appreciation to ourselves, others, and the resources entrusted to us. We should focus on building productive relationships, free from bullying and inappropriate behavior. A leader should create an environment where diverse perspectives and views are encouraged, expected, and valued. Because he is in a position of power, the wise leader will make a special effort to listen to the points of view of others and seek to understand them. The statement *"Let's discuss"* should not mean to the team members that their opinions will be discounted and that the leader will impose his.

Respecting the point of view of others does not mean that everybody is right. After a consultation, all inputs will be integrated but not all will be accepted. And that is fine. It is part of respect: providing advice and letting go of controlling the final version of everything. Respect should work both ways.

Leaders focus on solutions and building relationships. Leaders try to approach all stakeholders, even in times of conflict, with the objective of creating a better and more positive relationship. Yes, sometimes it will fail to work, and others will refuse to cooperate. Such is life; humans can be like that. In such cases, at a minimum, leaders control their own behavior.

Finally, let's always keep in mind that the project is not the toy of the project manager. There is a danger of going too far on the methodology side and becoming an advocate of our view of project management. We must remember that we are servant leaders, hired to deliver value for a client or an organization. In our decisions, including choices of methodology, we must serve the interests of the clients (assuming, of course, all is legal). The job of the project manager is often a balance between providing fearless advice, making strategic decisions, and faithfully implementing what the client requires. The more strategic a project is, the more complex and important it is to balance these elements in a respectful manner.

Fairness

Fairness is our duty to make decisions in an impartial and objective way. Our conduct must be free from competing self-interest, prejudice, and favoritism. Very often, a fair decision should pass the test of transparency. Unless there is a specific privacy requirement, the decision-making process should be transparent. The decisions must be rational, supported by fairness, and free of favoritism and discrimination.

A subtle form of discrimination may be found in the hiring of staff or resources. It may be tempting to hire clones of ourselves, with the same background and same thinking as we have, but this will just increase groupthink with the team, reduce the overall strength of the project team, and decrease the quality of the final results. Groupthink, according to the Merriam-Webster dictionary, is *"a pattern of thought characterized by self-deception, forced manufacture of consent, and conformity to group values and ethics[7]."*

A fair decision will do more than comply with values and ethics. It will convey good leadership, building credibility and trust and helping the project team to focus on delivering excellence. And, to be fair, we should proactively solicit the point of view of others and honestly consider their input in our decisions. A fair decision should be applicable to anybody, and be adapted to the context. The decision should also pass the test of disclosure. Of course, not all decisions should be made public, but a fair decision should still pass the test of disclosure.

Finally, we must be able to recuse ourselves if needed, or, at least, make a full disclosure of our personal interests. Even the perception of a conflict of interest can be a problem. Disclosure and recusing ourselves as needed solves most of these problems.

Honesty

Honesty is our duty to understand the truth and act in a truthful manner, both in our communications and our conduct.

As a leader, we create the tone at the top for our project. It is the responsibility of the project manager to create a work environment where it is possible to tell the truth, whether it be positive or negative. Otherwise, the leader will soon put himself in the dangerous position that every report sent to him is fully massaged to remove dangerous information— until, of course, it becomes impossible to remove the dangerous information, or the dangerous information comes to light on its own. It seems that, in life, secrets stay secret for only so long.

---

[7] Definition of Groupthink
http://www.merriam-webster.com/dictionary/groupthink

Honesty is an important part of project leadership. Sound governance and leadership practice requires you to be transparent and honest. This, of course, doesn't mean inappropriate disclosure of confidential information to the wrong stakeholders. But transparency and honesty are a very useful test. You should not do things that are only acceptable if others don't know about it. You should also refuse to lie. It is your job to tell the truth, even the hard truth.

Providing accurate information in a timely manner is a core strategic role of the leader. In designing a report, it is important to be strategic and support strategic thinking and decision-making. However, it is vital not to confuse this with hiding the truth. Unfortunately, there is only a thin line between the strategic selection of data and hiding information, and that line is very easy to cross. Remember that if there is an issue, from a strategic thinking and decision-making point of view, you want to have all information available as soon as possible. Quality decisions require accurate and timely information.

To summarize honesty, imagine the kind of relationship one would build if others cannot trust his truthfulness and he doesn't encourage others to be honest in their communication with him. We often hear that project managers spend a significant part of their time communicating. While doing so, honesty should be a core principle. Of course, honesty is always balanced by the privacy rights and requirements linked to the information. Honesty doesn't mean to freely communicate information that should be private.

Encourage honesty. Create a culture where people can talk to you, and tell you the truth. It will enhance your chance of success.

"Honesty is the first chapter in the book of wisdom.[8]" – Quote from Thomas Jefferson (1743-1826[9])

Conclusion

Values and ethics are not just a modern item on the governance checklist. They have a significant impact on the trust and reputation we build as a leader of projects. They should be demonstrated through our behavior and valued in analysis, discussion, strategic thinking, and decision-making.

---

[8] Quote from Thomas Jefferson - Quoteswave.com
http://www.quoteswave.com/text-quotes/63720
[9] Wikipedia - Thomas Jefferson
http://en.wikipedia.org/wiki/Thomas_Jefferson

CHAPTER 6

People in project management

Introduction

It is easy to view project management as processes, tools, techniques, and methodology. As we know, project management is defined as an activity performed to achieve an objective: a new product, a new service, a study or research, etc. A project is approved and launched to achieve an objective, and a person is assigned to manage that project.

A project management methodology will be implemented to achieve the objective efficiently and manage all the various processes included in a project. PMBOK includes the following aspects: scope, time, cost, quality, human resources, communications, project risk, procurement, and stakeholders. Templates will be completed and tasks assigned. Performance indicators will be established to measure success. They will include the achievement of the objective, as well as the schedule, cost, and quality of the project.

This is project management.

But did the methodology forget about people in project management?

The Human Resources

At first glance, it doesn't seem so. There is a process called *Human Resource Management*. Let's see what we can find in PMBOK on this topic.

> "Project Human Resource Management includes the processes that organize, manage, and lead the project team. The project team is comprised of the people with assigned roles and responsibilities for completing the project. It includes planning human resource, acquiring, developing and managing the project team.10"

This is the classic management view of humans: they are resources. At the business or at the project level, you need resources to achieve your objectives. These resources can be:

- Material: various physical assets;
- Information: knowledge and information;
- Financial: financial resource requirements and the funding schedule; or
- Human Resources: people required to complete the tasks.

Human resources are just one of the kinds of resources required. Human resources are defined in quantities, competencies, and availability. They can be viewed as assets, and at times they can become disposable assets.

In financial management, in which accountants and financial experts help a business achieve its objectives by providing financial advice, everything can be expressed in numbers. Financial management is an important part of managing all activities of an organization or project. It includes planning, business cases, accounting of operations,

---

10 Project Human Resource Management, PMBOK 5th edition, p. 255

financial reports, forecasting, internal controls, acquisitions and mergers, procurement, and audits. It is a numbers game. This is close to the ultimate world for simplifying everything to numbers.

Managing resources is also part of financial management. Resources can be acquired, used, and sold, so they can be shown in the financial statement of the organization. Organizations use the time of various persons to accomplish their objectives. This is why we have the label of *"human resources."*

Beyond financial management

For proper leadership, however, we should look beyond the financial view of resources. Human resources are people.

I was lucky enough to have a business professor at my university who understood this. He had a larger view of the world of business, and he constantly explained that everything we do in accounting relates to people. To pass accounting exams, it is likely true that focusing on numbers, standards, methodology, and formulas may be sufficient. If we want to excel as an accountant in the real world, however, and really understand financial statements, we have to see the people in the financial statements. He dared to say that every number of a financial statement can be associated with people.

As an example, an asset is bought from a vendor (a person), by an employee (a person) in the organization, and will be used by employees (people) to offer something to a customer (also a person). The banker and the investors are people (really!). If you think about it, you can relate every business process to a person. While that person may not be directly visible, it still remains that business processes don't exist for their own sake.

After all, organizations are created by and exist for humans. Without humans, why would we have accounting? Thus, it is important to keep in mind the importance of people when crunching numbers. Some critics, or cynics, may say that this is not always done, but it should be.

People in project management

Let's do the same exercise for project management. Can we think about the larger context? Can we think about the people involved in and impacted by the project? After all, without people on our dear Planet Earth, there would be no project management as we know it.

Let's think about the people in project management, looking at each area described by PMBOK.

The scope is defined to satisfy the need of a person, who can be internal or external to the organization. Someone will finance the project. The schedule must take into account the availability of the human resources, who are people. Stakeholders are people with various needs who will be impacted by the project.

Communication also happens between two or more people. It is not sufficient to create reports and emails to document the project file. Communicating is a complex activity between human beings. It has its own set of complexities, including various factors contributing to its success and failure. The message must be understood and a real connection made to communicate successfully. This is not merely a mechanical exercise, supported by tasks and technologies. A person is on the other end of the message.

Is a contract required for your project? Forms and documents will need to be completed. Yet procurement is more than a legal document. It describes an agreement between two persons. The contract may be written on behalf of two legal entities, but the work and discussion is still done by real humans.

The project team is more than a combination of resources acquired to complete the tasks. It is a group of human beings who will achieve together the ups and downs, success and failures of the project. They will work, innovate, solve issues, be disappointed, and celebrate together.

Maybe because they like simplicity, some experts prefer working only with computers and machines. This approach can work if you want a career as an expert, but it will be insufficient if you want to lead strategic and complex projects. It is very important for you as a strategic project leader to recognize and view people as the critical and primary asset to the project's success. This includes, of course, the team, but also the project sponsor, the users, and any other stakeholders who may be impacted by the project either now or in the future. You need people and their personal skills and motivation to help you and the project team succeed. The value-added contribution of the project will be measured by all those persons, not by a computer or a complex analysis in a spreadsheet.

Conclusion

Everything we do involves people. Keeping this in mind is essential for strong leadership. After all, a robot, a computer, or a machine does not require much leadership from its owner. It just performs the activity it was designed to do. (Maybe because of that, some experts prefer the simplicity of working only with computers and machines.)

As an essential part of the journey to develop leadership skills, it is important to fully integrate people in all activities. How we engage with them matters. It will have a powerful impact on the results and the success of the project.

CHAPTER 7

Team leadership

Introduction

In the previous chapters, we covered the personal dimension of leadership, which includes the knowledge required as a foundation, an overview of the leader as a person, and finally a discussion on values and ethics. All these elements are essential on your path to developing leadership skills and achieving better success in a dynamic world. Leadership is first a personal development journey. As a project manager, you will have to manage a team, small or large. This is where a focus on the leader as a person will become very useful. After all, the leader is part of the team, and someone who should have a significant influence on the team.

Of course, a project is rarely done alone, though it is possible to find projects, even very strategic ones, which are accomplished by one person. As always, project management is broad and applies to so many things, and it is important not to oversimplify the world of project management. Its diversity of application is part of its richness.

Most often, however, a team completes a project, and team leadership is an important role for the project manager. This is the leadership role most often discussed. The team can be tiny, small, medium, or large for an epic, billion-dollar project, so the approach and leadership style will need to be adapted and aligned to the size of the project team. There is no one-size-fits-all format in project management. It is impossible to compare the approach for a project consisting of a three-person team with a massive project of 5,000 team members. It would be inappropriate to transfer the best practice of one project to the very different context of the other.

Leadership of the team is important, and managing people is essential. Despite the one-person projects that exist, most projects involve a team. The ability to share a vision and influence a team to achieve a final, common success is crucial for a leader.

In this section, we will discuss the various roles involved in managing a project team, each of which is important for the success of the project. There is no one role that is always best and should be used at all times. All the roles are important. The constant challenge of leadership is to select the best one for each context.

Task management

The first role is obvious. A project manager must definitely be involved in task management. A project is divided into numerous tasks to be done, and if tasks are not completed as planned, it will have a significant impact on the success of the project. Delays will occur, costs will increase, and quality may be affected. Ultimately, it is very possible that the project itself will fail. As such, it is important to start with a strong plan and the ability to manage the completion of all tasks effectively.

Team management starts with assigning roles and tasks, monitoring progress, correcting problems, and providing feedback. A project manager must be a good coordinator of activities. He must understand the interaction between project tasks and the various constraints. It is impossible to succeed without effective task management, which will likely involve more than just assigning tasks in project management software.

This book is about leadership, but it would be dangerous to think that leadership without effective task management can lead to success. A project leader who cannot perform the role of task manager would be lost and would likely deliver few results, if any.

Beyond being a taskmaster

We want to raise the discussion and the role of the project manager a level above supervising tasks. Too often, the role of the project manager is reduced to being a taskmaster, managing tasks and nothing else. But being a project manager should involve more than planning and task management, monitoring activities, and issuing orders. These are important activities; however, they are not sufficient. The project manager must be a leader. A project manager should bring to the table:

- knowledge of a specific area (construction, engineering, music, software, graphic design, etc.),
- project management skills, and
- leadership skills.

Project managers often evolve exactly in this order: A person is good at a certain skill, and he would like to achieve more results and inherit more responsibilities. He then discovers and learns project management. While project management provides some substantial performance gain, often something is missing. Next come leadership skills. Leadership focuses on the ability to strategically lead, communicate with, and influence people. Results are better with a holistic view of project management. Many areas are improved when we appropriately consider the people in project management. The problems are clearer, and the solutions are easier to find.

The human side of the project team

Tasks are not completed on their own but are executed by a team of people. This is not like giving instructions to a machine or computer. Human beings bring their own complexity to the equation. When reading about project management, the process may feel like a machine for which our role is to ensure that it functions correctly. It's all too easy to forget the human side of business. We get so bogged down in the processes and procedures, the board meetings and balance sheets, that we forget business doesn't exist for its own sake. Business is about human beings. This is why it is important to remember the people in project management.

When dealing with people, we will always have to deal with the individuality of each person. Every person brings his or her knowledge, perspectives, and biases on the subject. Everyone also brings his or her emotions and personal motivation to the project.

Leadership includes the ability to influence others to achieve a common goal. A leader will impact other people's feelings and behavior and can influence the motivation and actions of the team members. Often, leadership is presented with management of tasks on one side and motivation on the other side. It is true that a leader also needs to be a motivator. Can we really have a *demotivator* who also claims to be a leader? Probably not! Unfortunately, it does happen. We have all seen people in leadership and management positions who can demotivate a whole team with their speech, behavior, and decisions.

Team leadership also requires strategic thinking and decision-making. At times, the team will need someone with a vision and the ability to solve problems and make decisions. The team will need someone who believes in them and in the project. Leadership at that point must include more than task management. Creating a vision, sharing a vision, and motivating the team are all part of being a strategic project manager.

Competency of the team

The role of a project manager includes ensuring that all tasks have a resource assigned, available, and with the appropriate competencies. The leader should have a global view of the competency needed to complete the project. Competency is often discussed at the individual level: for the leader and for each team member. A better and more strategic view looks at the competency for the team as a whole.

The leader is in a unique position, usually selected because of his skills, experience, and previous successes. He can play a big role in the success of the project, but no one can succeed alone. All parts of the team are required. Imagine if nobody is there to open the door to the building in the morning! It could completely paralyze a project or even an organization. Likewise, in today's world, computers and electricity are often very high on the list of essential resources. To stop all activities, you just need a computer network down or a lack of electricity.

In the end, it is the competency of the team as a whole that matters. It is together that you have the highest synergy. As a team leader, it is a great tool to develop a competency matrix for your project and optimize the resources assigned to the project based on this model.

The ideal scenario would include experienced and qualified resources for all tasks; however, this perfect scenario may remain an impossible dream. In reality, the value-added role expected from the leader includes being able to provide guidance and mentoring to team members. It would be odd if the project manager were not useful to team members in the execution of the project. If that is the case, why is he there? What kind of leadership is he bringing to the project?

The spotlight

While completing the project, the spotlight should be on the team, not on the leader. To enable success of the team and obtain the best from all members, never take the spotlight. Always give credit to your people. You will be surprised by what people can accomplish when you believe in them. As it is sometimes said, a conductor turns his back to the audience while the orchestra faces forward. Let all members perform and be proud of what they've accomplished. Setting aside the level of your position and acknowledging their work goes a long way toward building trust and morale.

As a leader, don't think of yourself as above, but rather among. To be credible, a leader must be part of the team. A leader must be useful to the team, not just in a hierarchical position that is comfortable for one and a burden to others.

A strategic project can be on the center stage of an organization. Let the spotlight shine on all team members. True leaders share credit and enable their team members to shine.

As a leader, give credit where it is due. Give credit to the work of your team.

A learning environment

Projects tend to be an ideal environment for learning and innovation. They are the opposite of repetitive operational activities. Managing a project with the expectation that everything has been fully defined and refined would be a limiting performance factor. Because of the unique and specific nature of each project, especially in a dynamic world, it is important for team management to create and maintain a learning environment.

The team members will work hard, but at times they will do things incorrectly. As a leader, it is important to create the proper environment for coaching and learning. This starts with providing clear instructions. Vague assignments are unlikely to deliver exactly what is required. The worst combination is a micro-manager with unclear instructions. This is almost a guarantee for failure, as team members do not have mindreading abilities.

Instead of blaming and pointing fingers, it is much better to create a constructive and safe learning environment. After all, we all were beginners once. Some bosses seem to have forgotten that. A bad boss does not tolerate imperfection, as defined by him, and he may even lose his temper and become disrespectful. While this may feel good for the boss, it is deadly for group morale and is a terrible way to lead a team.

It is far more powerful to respect team members and, as a leader, create a learning environment for the team. At times, yes, you will have to correct errors and redirect effort. Others have had to do that for you, and you as the leader will continue learning for the rest of your life. There is no end to learning. This applies both to you as a leader and to your team.

 If you create an innovative and dynamic work environment, instead of a rigid one defined by social class (the manager, the supervisor, the workers, etc.), it will make an enormous difference in the performance of and value added by your project. Done the right way, everybody grows in the process, and the quality of the end result is higher.

Failure is unavoidable on the path to learning and achieving success. Thomas Edison (1847-1931[11]) is quoted as saying when trying to invent the light bulb:

> "I have not failed. I've just found 10,000 ways that won't work.[12]"

Failing is part of learning. There is no way to innovate and succeed without a certain possibility of failure. Status quo is the only way to not fail, and then one would fail in a different way. Status quo brings obsolescence very quickly in today's world. As such, in a dynamic world, some organizations like to design processes to accelerate failure, in order to be able to learn from it. Ultimately, one should always value the silver lining of failure: the lessons learned.

When a project fails, the temptation is always to find something to blame, to point the finger at someone, and to deflect criticism away from ourselves. But blaming isn't productive. People are already disappointed by the failure, and adding blame will only worsen the harm and destroy our ability to learn and exploit opportunities. With each failure, you learn something you didn't know before, or discover strength you didn't know you had.

A learning environment is one of the most powerful tools one can use to succeed in a dynamic environment, where innovation and changes are so rapid and constant.

Keep the mood positive

Groups always work better together inside a positive work and social environment. That is why we had a chapter on the leader first, which included information on self-awareness and de-stressing. It may be possible at times to obtain a higher level of performance with stress, by raising

---

[11] Wikipedia - Thomas Edison
http://en.wikipedia.org/wiki/Thomas_Edison
[12] Quote from Thomas Edison - Quoteswave.com
http://www.quoteswave.com/picture-quotes/15402

alarm and increasing the panic level of individuals on the project, but it is only a short-term gain, with long-term negative impacts.

Besides, this manufactured stress is often an inaccurate description of reality. It is like screaming *"fire"* for nothing. After a while, nobody will listen. Not all issues are critical, life-threatening, and must be solved within 7.5 minutes. Ultimately, if a project is always managed in panic and stress mode, it is most likely a symptom of a much larger problem. At some point, as a leader, it is much better to fix the root cause of a problem than to only try to manage the symptoms.

As much as possible, let's create a positive work environment. In a project, if the mood in the main office is positive, people will be much more productive than if the mood is negative.

This starts with the mood that the leader brings to the workplace every morning. A lot of what determines the quality of the work environment of an organization is the leader and the extent to which he or she cultivates this positive mood. People who see a reason to be optimistic about their work situation will be more productive, and the morale in the office will improve. It's every bit as much an upward spiral as a negative mood is a downward one.

After all, it is not really reassuring to the team members if the project manager is stressed, unhappy, and not confident about the success of the project. Even if he is unhappy for personal reasons, it is still going to have an impact on the team.

What if the situation is dire? What if there's no reason to remain confident? Don't people deserve to be told the truth? Sure they do. But it's all in how you frame things. First, don't confuse issues with people. A situation or a project may be in trouble and failing, but not the team members. Give people a reason to see the positive side. Put forward a plan to solve the problem, and ask for their cooperation in setting the plan in motion. Keep people informed, and keep them feeling like they are part of a team, and you have begun the first steps in an upward spiral toward success.

Empathy

In team leadership, empathy is another essential component. You have to be able to understand the context, perspective, and point of view of others. It is too easy to see everything only from our own perspectives. It is easy to be convinced that we know the whole truth; it is much harder to have a comprehensive view of the situation.

Reality is often complex and requires the ability to view it from various angles. The perspectives of others will provide significant insight into the project or situation and will provide a much better basis for decision-making. Ultimately, correctly understanding the complexity of facts and situations will have a significant impact on the success of the project.

Empathy will enable a leader to understand the various stakeholders correctly, at an authentic level. Stakeholder management requires a sincere understanding of each of their perspectives. This is not just a template to be completed, as provided by the project management office. Empathy will help a leader to better understand the client and project sponsor.

Empathy will also help you manage your team effectively. A bad leader will discard the idea of giving due consideration to the work environment of the team members. He will not correctly assess the level of stress of the team. He may dismiss the importance of issues or support required to resolve them. Sometimes the correct answer is to push the team to do more; sometimes they truly have too much to do. Sometimes you have to push team members to solve issues; sometimes they do need to escalate and have your support as the leader.

Lack of empathy from the leader weakens results. Empathy is not an optional soft skill; it is an essential skill for a leader. Remember that as a leader, you have the responsibility of showing strength. You have to be there when it is difficult. You cannot abandon ship at a difficult time or panic when facing difficulties.

Here is a simple example. If a project requires overtime, remember that as a leader you also are part of the project team. You are not a fixture, or a mailbox, sending instructions to others. Must the team work over the weekend to complete an important work package? Be there with the team! Be the first to arrive on the weekend and the last to leave.

A leader must be able to see the perspectives of others, including team members, clients, project sponsors, stakeholders, and other members of the organization. Don't be too quick to judge, and don't be too fast to refute the arguments of others. They have a different point of view, often based on their positions, which gives them a different perspective.

Sit down, shut up, and listen. Are you able to explain the opinion of the other person, without providing any judgment and refutation? If not, then as a leader you do not yet understand the perspectives of the other person. You must remove your ego and become more of a servant leader. You are there as a project manager to accomplish a goal, and unless you are doing a project for yourself, you are mandated by someone else to accomplish it. Don't become too emotional about everything, turning it into a *"my way or no way"* situation. Show people that you care about their needs.

Effective coordination

In managing a project team, effective coordination will have a powerful impact on the cost, length, and quality of the project. Lack of coordination will lead to inefficiencies, increased timelines, and most likely increasing costs.

Transparency in the project plan is useful to everyone. Even if some team members only participate in one component of the plan, it is best to share with them as much of the approved plan as possible. They will better understand the relationships between each part and feel less that deadlines are just artificial dates. They can also become proactive and suggest ways to perform the project plan differently and better. When they have a complete view of the plan, they may even say that they can start a new task if they have more availability.

Transparency of information is extremely powerful. The team becomes more focused on completing the tasks and less on waiting passively for the next assignment or team meeting. This is why information management in a project is so important, even though, unfortunately, it is so often overlooked. Transparent information ensures that everybody on the team is working based on the same set of information and is spending less time creating status reports.

A good leader will demonstrate that he correctly understands the workload and won't create impossible solutions, delegations, and assignments. Sometimes rich sponsors think that you can just throw more resources at a problem to solve it. This may be the case, or it may not. As in the famous example, nine women cannot give birth to one baby in one month.

This is one of the benefits of project management and team collaboration applications, ideally online applications. They make the information easily accessible and visible to all team members. They make project reports easy to prepare and provide a solid foundation for decision-making. In addition, with the team collaboration features, discussion related to a task is available to all, not just stored in the email inbox of some of the team members. Team members do not need to be interrupted to obtain an update. The information is available and shared.

Visibility of project information is one of the great benefits of online project management and team collaboration applications. For some, it is also the key reason they don't like it. You can no longer filter information and adjust the report; the truth is visible. But as leaders, we should not be afraid of visibility.

Virtual Teams

Project management now often involves virtual teams. At first, this can be viewed as a challenge. Isn't it easier to have everybody in the same room, working the same 9 to 5? In some ways, this is true. But virtual teams also force you as a project manager to develop good management habits.

In this day and age, having remote members on your team is becoming the norm rather than the exception. The project doesn't need team members located in different countries and time zones to have a virtual team. You may just need someone in a different building on the same site, or even on a different floor. You don't need team members across the world to experience the new challenges of a virtual team. They are the same for telework and dispersed teams in operation. At first it is a challenge, but it is also an opportunity.

Is it that bad or difficult? It shouldn't be. In the end, we are supposed to manage results, not monitor time or presenteeism. No project was ever successful simply because the project manager could monitor team members sitting on chairs near him.

As a leader, you don't need to control every minute of your employees' work. Work should not feel like community work, where you have to be present and mark your time. Performance management is not about presence management. Work is a matter of achieving results. A key requirement to effectively manage a virtual team is to align the team to the work objectives. If, at the end of the day, you cannot control your team members' work by assessing the results they are achieving, then you need to improve your delegation skills.

Virtual teams are often an opportunity. If managed correctly, they will enhance the contribution of every member to the project. It may be at first a challenge, and you will have to be strategic and communicate very clearly to team members. While it may feel like a burden, it is actually a powerful learning experience for the leader, and the leader should be grateful for it.

What strategies will you use to help your virtual team members feel more connected? You need to delegate and clarify the work to be done. You need to empower team members to have ideas and contribute. Because virtual teams require you to master delegation and communication, I actually find that learning to manage a virtual team will actually make you a better manager of any team, including a *"normal"* collocated team.

Conclusion

In the end, the team is your asset to achieve the best quality results possible. Don't expect your team members to look up to you if you look down on them. As a leader, you will set the tone for the work environment of the project. You need to have a sense of humor. You will have issues, problems, seagull management, bad stakeholders, bad team members, and perfect storm events. Despite all attempts to plan everything, you will have to deal with reality[13]. Like they say in the military, it is important to plan, but plans never survive the reality of the battlefield. You are also providing an example for your team; if in difficult times you become tense, rigid, stressed, intellectual, or introverted, you will reduce the contribution of the whole team.

Strategic and complex projects require leadership, and the leader will have a significant impact on the team. Leadership should provide a vision to the team, as well as direction and motivation. A leader should be supportive and carry the team successfully to its destination during difficult times. In all cases, support the team members. Don't *throw them under the bus* for your own selfish career interests.

Your team is one of your most precious and powerful assets to succeed. You must believe in them.

---

[13] For the curious, seagull management is a management style. The term became popular through a joke in the book "Leadership and the One Minute Manager" by Ken Blanchard, published in 1985. As it says in the book, "Seagull managers fly in, make a lot of noise, dump on everyone, then fly out".
http://en.wikipedia.org/wiki/Seagull_manager

CHAPTER 8

Delegation

Sharing the work

It is impossible to discuss team leadership without at some point touching on the subject of delegation. At one extreme, we find one-person projects. In these, delegation is not an issue. One person will do it all, from strategic thinking, to creating a plan, executing the tasks, monitoring progress, and closing the project. However, to be honest, most projects will involve a team of some size, and sometimes a very large one. The leader is responsible for the execution and coordination of all activities. As such, he has a crucial role in ensuring that effective delegation is done.

Delegation is broader than project management. As someone gets more responsibilities and promotions, he will have a team and more work to do than he can do alone. There is a ceiling on what any human being can accomplish within a specific period of time, so you have to learn to delegate if you want to be able to lead, get a promotion, and be successful at higher levels.

Delegation is not done with the goal of you, the project manager, doing nothing and enjoying a nice, comfortable position. Project manager would then be a useless overhead position. The project manager is part of the team and must contribute something beyond simply being a mailbox. Also, it is important to never ask someone to do something that you're unwilling to do yourself. That is not the purpose of delegation.

You must take advantage of all the abilities of a team in order to maximize the contribution of all members of the team. If you are trying to do too much on your own, quality will slip, and you will start to miss deadlines. This is a sign that you need to delegate more.

Delegation is about optimization of the workload, maximizing results, and efficiency.

Project context

An Internet search on delegation will reveal many articles on the subject. Often, they will include a simple, magic recipe for delegation. However, the reality of projects is too diverse and complex to be simplified in such a way.

Delegation is hard to address without first knowing the context of the project. A small, three person project will not have a separate project management team, and everybody will have to contribute in completing tasks. An epic construction project – such as building the bridge to Prince Edward Island in Canada or between Malmo and Copenhagen, or heading the construction of the 2,460-meter (8,070 ft) Millau Viaduct in the Pyrénées in France – will have a distinct project management team solely dedicated to assigning tasks, monitoring progress, preparing reports, meeting stakeholders, managing finances, and coordinating activities. Because each project has its own context and level of complexity, advice on delegation can range from excellent to overly simplified, or just inappropriate.

Let's start with the basics. The first requirement for delegation is having too much for one person to do. Since the project is all about delivering a result, if you don't have too much work for one person, the person completing the work is essential, and the other is a burden on the project.

The second requirement is that you have a team to which you can delegate. The lack of human resources to complete the project would be a significant and strategic issue which must be discussed with the project sponsor. It would not be appropriate to move forward with a project which is doomed from the beginning due to a lack of resources.

Delegation is interesting: there is the problem of not enough of it and the problem of too much of it. On one hand, there is the hero syndrome, with a project manager trying to do everything on his own; on the other hand, there is the mailbox syndrome, where the manager adds no value to the project and acts merely as a taskmaster above the project team.

A key responsibility of a strategic project leader is to understand fully and accurately the context of his project. This is one of the keys to success. It will help in making wise decisions and avoiding the pitfalls of blindly applying concepts which are irrelevant to the current context of the project.

How to delegate

Often, advice on delegation assumes that you are a micro-manager control freak who wants everything done your own way, and that you have a large team. Your team is under-utilized, and you are overwhelmed. That is, of course, a very inappropriate way to delegate. Delegation should result in achieving more by maximizing the contribution of all team members. It enables the project to benefit from the competencies of the whole team. Delegation is more than sharing tasks. It creates synergies within the team.

As one gets a promotion, or manages larger project teams, he has to become strategic. He has to learn to let go. At first, it may be hard. It is often hard. It is such a challenge that too often managers blame the employees, when delegation can also be a problem for them. But once this barrier is crossed, the results are surprising.

Delegation is a way to share responsibility and get more work done when the sum of the work to be done is bigger than what one person can do. How much delegation is required is a matter of equilibrium between work and resources. As such, it is not correct to say that you should delegate every task, and that you are only paid to do work as a project manager. That depends on the project complexity and the work that needs to be done. In a small project, the project manager is definitely part of the team doing the tasks. At the extreme, in a project of one, the project manager is the team, managing and doing all tasks. At the other extreme, a large project with a big team, complexity, and a lot of integration requirements will need a project manager solely focusing on managing and monitoring the project, as well as coordinating communication with stakeholders. Even managing the project management team will be a significant task for large projects.

When you delegate, you must clarify what kind of delegation you are doing: task or empowerment, creativity or procedural execution? Even if you want to delegate a task entirely, it fits somewhere in the vision of the project and of the sponsor. The leader must always clearly communicate his strategic vision for the work to be done. Another critical element is to make the person aware of the connections. Why do you need such a work, completed by that date? Why do you value this requirement in your strategic vision of the task? Expecting mind reading from others is an ineffective way to communicate and ensure success of your project. Communicating requirements only during the final part of the project is a very bad way to manage! It does not lead to a pragmatic solution and is a sign of bad leadership.

When you delegate, you should focus on results and not on managing time, and then assess how much support the person needs to complete the task. A design task will require more interaction than a simple operational task, for example.

Proper delegation requires trust, honesty, respect, and good communication. An email forwarded without instructions may leave the receiver unclear as to what needs to be done. In addition, when you delegate, you have to learn to let go. You want to achieve an objective, of course, but there are many different ways to achieve a goal. Sometimes your way is correct, and you should act as a mentor. Sometimes the other approach is different but just as good. When it is just different, let it go. The other approach may even be better. Quality is not a tool to protect your ego. Enjoy the fact that team members are contributing alongside you.

The value-added role of the project manager

Delegation optimizes the contribution of every member of the project team, including — not excluding — the project manager. Leaders should be part of the team, not above it. *"Leader"* is not a position; it is a role. Leadership is not a social class, a comfortable chair with no duties. The leader has to bring value to the project.

When delegating, the leader should provide value to the process. He should delegate, not dictate or abdicate. He should be more than a mysterious, aloof boss, not understanding the tasks and not being able to provide any useful support.

After all, the project manager is part of the team and part of the cost of the human resources assigned to the project.

He should not just be a mailbox, someone receiving instructions from others and sending them back to the team, receiving status updates and sending them back to stakeholders. Like all other team members, he must contribute to the project. Failing that, he is just a mailbox. And how much do you think the project sponsor, or even better, the client, should pay for a mailbox?

The mailbox syndrome happens when a project manager delegates too much and is adding no value to the project, thus becoming only an overhead cost. Everybody will know it sooner or later, and it will have an adverse impact on the cost of the project and on the team, who will not feel supported and will not see the value-added role of the leader.

Delegation is required in the presence of too many tasks, but when delegating, you should still be able to add value. You must focus on the strategic roles of the project manager, in which you add the most value to the project. This is done by providing strategic direction, support, and mentoring if needed. The leader can also help by providing horizontal integration with other units in the project and with key stakeholders. Along with all this, it is important to value and believe in the team and not become obsessed with our own way of doing things.

Stretch goals

In a dynamic world, you want to embed learning, agility, and flexibility into the design of your organization. This also applies to the project team. In such a dynamic world, the status quo costs more than learning. A key way to learn is to give stretch assignments to your team members. Make sure that everybody can contribute to the project and learn from their participation.

Most people like to feel like they are progressing, learning, growing. If they feel they are improving, they are more engaged and more likely to contribute. Thus, offering opportunities to advance and develop is one of the main responsibilities of a leader. As a leader, it's necessary to find goals that push the group, but not to an unachievable level. Finding such a goal is one of the creative pleasures of the leader.

You may have someone in your group who isn't performing and who you think doesn't deserve such a stretched path until he proves that he can meet the standard. But I suggest looking at the situation another way. Those people might not believe in themselves, and they need to know that someone does believe in them. Maybe they don't take the initiative because they previously suffered under bad leadership.

There is a fine line between being realistic and assessing the reality. The danger is in making reality conform to your assessment. It has been proven many times in psychology that if you believe that someone cannot do something, your belief will create that reality by setting limits on that person. As a leader, make sure not to become a constraint with your own assessment of your team members. As a leader, you have to be the person who believes the most in your team.

Poor performance

Of course, at times, you may have to address performance issues. However, you should get to this point only after having done your best to develop all team members. After all, team member performance is a function of what both the supervisor and the employees bring to the equation. It is too easy to assign blame, especially when we are in a position of power. An integrated approach requires assessing the performance of both the manager and the employees. This is not easy, and there is no simple answer.

Still, it will happen that a team member will not perform at the required and expected level. If all else has been done, then the poor performance must be addressed. It is important to find the courage to have those discussions with the person. Not doing so will impact the leadership, the trust, and the reputation of the leader for the regular and high-performing team members, as they will wonder why there is a double standard. We all know those organizations in which most people must meet performance levels, except one or a few people, and nobody is doing anything about it.

These discussions must be held as early as possible. They must be authentic and non-judgmental, focused on solutions. It is also useful to properly identify the root cause of the problem. It will help to create a useful and doable action plan to solve the problem. The steps in the action plan should be small and doable. Progress is done one step at a time. Asking for a gigantic leap forward will likely be destructive, creating an impossible plan full of fear which will become a cause of discouragement.

If the employee refuses to address the problem, it should be clear that it is his sole decision, and that all possible tools and support were provided to him. Surely, if the team member refuses to or cannot improve performance, it is essential to have the courage to take final action for the good of the project.

Conclusion

Delegation is a constant challenge as one gets more promotions and is assigned to more complex and strategic projects. As such, it is a critical skill for leadership. It is important to properly develop delegation skills; otherwise, this will be a very limiting factor in your career.

Delegation should be about optimization of work. All members, including the project manager, should contribute and add value to the project. How this occurs depends on the context and complexity of the project. To properly learn delegation, you have to constantly assess and answer the following questions:

- What is the context and complexity of the project?
- What are the tasks and workload required in the project?
- What way is best to optimize delegation based on the skills of each team member?

In managing delegation, it is important to create a learning environment. It is also important to ensure that we as project managers have a value-added role in the project. What that role will be depends on the context and complexity of the project, as well as the tasks required. There is no one-size-fits-all solution. The world of project management is too broad and diverse for that.

CHAPTER 9

Strategic thinking

The strategic leader

If project management is to be a useful strategic tool in organization, then project managers must learn to think and act at that level. Project management should not just be an administrative and tactical tool. Yes, the methodology includes many tools, processes, and techniques, but as a leader, it is important to think a level above this and be strategic. Otherwise, the project manager is only a taskmaster, diligently supervising tasks during all phases of the project. Doing so limits the value added by the project manager and leaves the strategic thinking to someone else. It is always best to be a strategic project leader, as this will enhance our value for our clients. This should not be viewed as a luxury or left completely to others.

Project management is rarely boring. Often, our projects keep us very busy, and our world is full of activity, dynamic, and constantly evolving. But it is not okay to be busy without a larger plan. As a leader, you must take the time to step back, reflect, think strategically, and create a vision. Managing tasks can certainly keep the project manager busy, but without strategic thinking he may end up being busy with no or very little result.

Strategic thinking is fundamental in leadership. While a leader should be able to influence others and motivate the team, if he doesn't have a strategy, he reduces his role to one of cheerleading. Leadership without strategic thinking and decision-making would be very limited.

To maximize our efficiency as leaders, we must be strategic, bringing vision, strategic analysis, and decision making to our project. We must be someone who the team, the sponsor, and other key stakeholders can rely on for our thinking and judgment. They all want and benefit from having a project manager who can play at the strategic level and thus add maximum value to the project.

Vision

To play the complete role of a leader, it is important to understand the why of the project. The strategic vision must be developed with a deep understanding of the end results and why the project matters. You must be able to communicate this vision of the project in a compelling way.

This vision is rarely given to you crystal-clear in the project charter as something imposed on you by others. Still, part of the vision will come to you in that way, since we often lead projects on behalf of others. Unless you are the owner and president of your company, you do not complete the project ultimately for yourself.

Remember, the project sponsor is looking for the value in the project. The methodology is only a tool to deliver that value. Go in-depth strategically in understanding the business case behind the project. Make sure you understand why it was approved, even before the project initiation phase. It is much better to understand the full life cycle of the deliverables, even after the closing phase of the project.

It is very important to understand and respect the goals and perspectives of the clients. The project manager is hired to manage the project of someone else (unless, again, you manage a project for yourself), so he should practice servant leadership. Servant leadership is both a philosophy and set of leadership practices. Traditional leadership generally involves the accumulation and exercise of power by one at the *"top of the pyramid."* By comparison, the servant-leader shares power, puts the needs of others first, and helps people develop and perform to their best.

Receiving the vision of others should not stop our inspiration to add and contribute to the vision, however. At the minimum, we must be able to provide ideas and advice, even fearless advice. The vision can and should be developed with the involvement of your team, if possible. The vision will be richer and have more depth, and the team will likely be more engaged and attached to its success. The final vision will be the strategic integration of all these inputs.

Whatever the final vision is, including a few or many of your thoughts and possibly the thoughts of others, you then have to be a servant leader and be completely aligned with it. You have to believe in this vision. There is no place for *"Well, they want us to do this, so we have to do it."*

It is often said that communication is one of the most important roles of a project manager. As such, communicating the vision of the project is essential. You must be able to communicate it not only to your project team, but also to the sponsor, internal stakeholders, and external stakeholders. A leader will bring cohesion between team members and other stakeholders around the vision. He will help articulate the benefits of the project, the reason for its existence, and clear objectives and milestones.

At all times, the leader should own the vision and be the first to be proud of the project, as well as help others embrace this vision with enthusiasm.

Holistic thinking for strategy

Too often, I have seen great ideas proposed and quickly adopted as strategies without sufficient research and analysis to validate the concept and identify all the requirements. Strategies without good implementation are only a dream; it is with actions that we accomplish and create something. The full sequence for success includes:

- **Vision:** identification of the goal of the project, its benefits and why it matters,
- **Strategy:** analysis of requirements and options and selection of a strategy to implement the vision, and
- **Implementation:** actions taken to implement the strategy and achieve the vision.

As a leader, you should completely understand the rationale and expected benefits of the project. Be sure to ask enough questions to understand the why behind the project. What problem are we trying to solve? What is the opportunity justifying this project? Why is it important? Who is it important to? Do not trust that the initial discussions and the project charter will reveal all the information, and do not think that the performance indicator of the project tells the full story.

We have here a fundamental difference between project leadership and project management. In project management, if you have delivered exactly what has been requested, you have done your job. In project leadership, you focus on the value added proposition of the project.

Managing strategically

As mentioned earlier, leading a project requires more than just motivating a team and supervising tasks. Project leadership requires the project manager to manage strategically throughout the life of the project. This should not be reserved only for the initial planning phase. The vision is the goal of the project; strategic thinking is the direction for its successful implementation.

As an example, strategic thinking is required to handle ideas, changes, and innovations during the project. As the project progresses, the team may propose new ideas and new ways of doing things. Change requests to the project scope may be received from various stakeholders. How do you decide if they should be approved? If you don't understand the project from a strategic point of view, all changes become a battle between the initial project documentation and a revised documentation. If you understand the fundamental why of the project, then some changes may be welcome, as they will increase the value proposition of a project.

Strategic analysis should be comprehensive, yet rapid and decisive. It should be anchored in the vision of the project and supported with a proper understanding of its strengths and weaknesses, threats and opportunities. Is an idea proposed to solve a problem? While assessing the idea, find as many downsides as possible. Identify the point of failure, not to become paranoid and paralyzed, but to optimize the plan and enhance the probability of success. Challenge your assumptions and identify what can go wrong. If the point of failure may be a significant problem, a leader must make sure that it is on his monitoring screen and that he is ready to react and make decisions as quickly as possible if issues arise.

In the strategic analysis and leadership of the project, it is important to have a larger perspective and understand the impact of the project on other projects or activities in the organization. Of course, these impacts may be related and part of managing the business requirements of the project. However, the strategic leaders should have a broader view of the project. He should understand where the project fits in the portfolio of activities of the organization.

To be a strategic leader, it is essential to look at the big picture, and evaluate the impact of a decision on all other activities. Will it slow down other tasks, or other projects? The opportunity cost is a very powerful concept to understand. Whenever we decide to do something, we also decide not to do something else. Some decisions close doors on other potential strategies, while others keep options open.

In a dynamic world, options are gold. Let's suppose that you have the choice between two decisions, and both are equivalent. Option A gives you options for future decisions. Option B is a closed path. If you are in a dynamic environment, managing a complex project, you should prefer option A. That is why in the world of finance, options have a value. As a leader, you should embed as many options as possible in your project plan.

Strategic thinking should be supported by a comprehensive analysis and sufficient data. It is also important to ensure that the analyses are sufficiently broad and in-depth. A variety of skills and backgrounds is required, so it is easier to prepare a comprehensive analysis with the support of others. Their knowledge and experience will give them a different perspective which will enrich the overall analysis. This is like a game of chess, in which it is always interesting to see different players analyzing the same positions. The board is the same. The position of pieces is the same. Everyone perceives it the same way. Everybody works from the same set of information, yet different players will see different options in a position. In chess, experts will see things on the board that less advanced players will not see.

Likewise, in a project, the view of experts should be appropriately considered. They will detect things you don't see. If you learn to listen to them, you will enhance your chance of success. Ignoring them will increase the blind spots of the project plan and of you as the leader of the project.

Do you have people on your team who can disagree with you and provide an alternative perspective? Be careful of those who only agree with you, who always claim that everything is progressing fine. Of course, it requires a high level of professionalism to disagree respectfully, and it is also essential to be able to provide advice and let go of the final decision. This is well summarized in this principle: *"Fearless advice, faithful implementation."*

Blind spots of leadership

Leadership has a paradox. On one hand, the leader often has a larger and more global view of the project, giving him more information than others. On the other hand, he is more remote from the activities of the project, creating blind spots. The bigger your project team, the more this paradox will be at play. With large teams, the leader will be farther away from the project activities and will be unable to see and know everything that is happening.

Leadership can be an interesting role, but sometimes it comes with its own inconveniences, and one of them is the distance from the project activities. Sometimes leaders think that they know and control everything, but that is an illusion, which only works because they are in a bubble.

It is wise for leaders to go beyond this naive approach and accept the existence of these blind spots. A wise leader is aware of blind spots and tries to reduce them as much as possible. This will give him a more accurate view of reality and provide better support for strategic thinking and decision-making.

The first solution to these blind spots is going out of the bubble. There is a good, old concept called managing by walking around. It is important to understand your project, its context, and what the team is doing. You have a project that relates to airports? Go visit an airport. Your project is to organize a conference? Visit the conference room in advance. From time to time, go and visit various activities. You want to see what it is like for your employees to apply the processes of the organization, so try it out yourself. Get out of the corporate office, get out of meetings, and see the work being done.

I promise you two things: It will be a humbling experience, and it will also be an extremely powerful learning experience. You will learn so much by doing this that you will wonder how anyone can really be a leader while hiding in the comfort of his office. Wise leaders know the risks of being disconnected from the operations. Strategic thinking without a good understanding of the details can destroy a project.

Naturally, project reports can fill some of this information gap, but a report is always only a summary of the reality. It simplifies reality, just like a map simplifies the terrain, and it may not always tell the full truth. Also, reports rarely describe the work environment, the feelings of team members, and the beat of the floor. Even worse, a perfect report may hide a perfect storm by burying it under a mountain of positive thinking. Unfortunately, the report doesn't change reality. Sooner or later, the problems will be visible.

As a project manager, you are paid to manage. To avoid blind spots, you need to make sure the people around you are going to give you all the facts. Not just the good, not just what you want to hear, not just what they think you want to hear. To be comfortable in sharing the truth, telling you the good and the bad news in a timely manner, they must feel that you will listen in a respectful and non-judgmental way.

Are you compelling your team members to disclose their challenges? Are you seeking that information in team meeting discussions? Are you doing it in a non-judgmental way? Be their partner and ally in resolving difficulties.

Encourage open communication to ensure ideas are discussed. Solicit feedback and ask a lot of questions. Be strategic with your actions and communication. You have to create an environment safe for the truth.

The strategic use of lessons learned

Lessons learned is a concept often heard, but not always performed. If it is performed, it may not be done in a strategic manner, but rather with the intention of completing a process and complying with the methodology.

What are lessons learned? They are all the knowledge gained during a project which shows how events were addressed or should be addressed in the future, with the purpose of improving future performance. Discussing and documenting the lessons learned is one of the key processes to be completed while closing the project. The most active use of lessons learned takes place in large and complex projects. To reduce risk, these projects are frequently executed in an iterative fashion by allowing the team to incorporate feedback and lessons learned between iterations. Projects can often benefit from lessons learned in previous projects. In agile methodology, the retrospective review would include lessons learned for correcting and improving processes, if required.

Gathering lessons learned is a forgotten art in project management. The idea is that the organization should have knowledge bases, such as lessons learned and historical information, which the project manager can consult in the planning phase to develop the best possible project plan. It is a great concept that I have rarely seen developed and used in a methodical way.

Lessons learned should be part of leadership. Mental agility, as I call it, is the ability to constantly grow and change our way of thinking. The opposite is dogma. It is best to stay away from dogmas of any kind, including those from education and experience. Dogmas can sometimes be the consequence of success. Because a leader did something this way in the past, it has to be done the same way in the future. Repetition is easy; it takes great leadership to be able to tell your team that something will be done differently this time, even if last time your decision was not the same.

This is a potential downside of success: it can reduce the mental space allowed for thinking and innovation. You can see this with experts who sell the same idea for thirty years, a bit like an overextended movie franchise. In some ways, this is why it is beneficial to hire periodically from outside the organization, to get fresh new ideas. There must be a balance between internal promotion and bringing in external ideas. This is also why someone at the helm of the same unit or company for a long time may start to have blind spots, unless he cultivates the art of mental agility. After all, everything in the unit has been developed under his leadership.

It is creative destruction, as Schumpeter[14] would say. Don't fall in love with the way you delivered the project and the decisions you made before. It will kill all hopes for identifying better ways, new ideas, and opportunities for improvements. Make the strategic choice of infinite and constant learning for mental agility.

Conclusion

A project manager who wants to be a leader must fully play the role. He must go beyond merely managing tasks and motivating the team to bring strategic thinking to the projects he is managing. This is one of his most value-added contributions.

---

[14] http://en.wikipedia.org/wiki/Joseph_Schumpeter

Strategic thinking helps the project manager set goals, identify threats and opportunities, analyze options, allocate resources, and determine priorities. Developing strategic thinking is essential to becoming a strategic project leader and providing the most value to the project.

CHAPTER 10

Project management in a dynamic world

A paradigm shift

Project management methodology is often based on the assumption that the project is an isolated activity or change in a very stable environment. This was probably true in the past, during the 20th century. Even not too long ago, this assumption was probably accurate and valid, so much that it was pointless to even discuss it. The stability of the environment was the natural order, not worthy of being discussed, just as we don't discuss the presence of air on Earth when preparing a project. It is there, and we can take it for granted.

This mindset is evident in the way we describe changes. They are something to be managed in order to help an organization move from A to B. The assumption is that A was the previous stable environment, and B will be the new stable environment. In that environment, project management can be managed like a machine. You can plan everything and it should work almost automatically, in a very predictable manner.

On the other hand, we now have an environment filled with constant and rapid changes. The pace of innovation is constantly accelerating. Just think of the gap in technology from 1975 to 1985, and then to 1995, and finally from 2005 to 2015. It is so fast that many children in today's world cannot imagine a world without computers. Once I was explaining to one of my sons about the days of the first personal computers, in the 80s when I was a teenager. He then asked me:

> "What computer were you using before the first computer?"

So we have a massive paradigm shift: the environment is moving from a stable place to a very dynamic world. What are the impacts of that change on project management and the role of the project manager?

The machine

Project management can be viewed as a machine. If only we would use the machine correctly and feed it with the perfect information, there would be no issues. With this approach, the role of the project manager is to make sure that all the processes and tools are used and followed so the project will succeed.

At times, it may feel that the role of the project manager is simply appointed to ensure that the project is in compliance with project management methodology. Success, as measured by the client, becomes a secondary measure. In this view, the role of the project manager is a coordinator and an enforcer. He coordinates tasks to ensure that work packages are complete, as per requirements and project methodology. I like to describe this role as the Taskmaster.

With the advance of artificial intelligence, computer power, and software, I often get the feeling that maybe in an ideal world, we could program a computer to be a project manager. Just enter all the project specifications, including the approved work plan, and the computer will execute in the proper order all the various tasks until the completion of the project.

This is the beauty of the perfect project documentation. You get a good understanding of the requirements, develop a plan, and then execute the plan as defined and approved. Assuming you have done your homework and properly defined the plan, everything should happen as planned.

This is the beauty of a Gantt chart. It will tell you in perfect harmony who will do what and when. You can look at the plan, and it will tell you that Joe will do this on October 21, and Jane will be working on that on November 1. All dependencies have been considered and effort required has been analyzed, along with leads and lags in the timeline.

The reality

On the other hand, reality is often a lot more complex. There is no such thing as a perfect plan and perfect execution. It is important to always understand what a document means and what it doesn't mean, and a Gantt chart is a good example of this. It may give you the illusion of controlling the universe, telling you when everyone is going to work on what. While a very useful tool, it is important to remember that it is an approximation of the reality, just like a map is only a simplification of the terrain.

Despite all the tools and techniques available, project managers must be able to manage reality. To do that, you must be able to have a good view on the facts as they are. Our perception of reality may be inaccurate, yet our minds are good at believing that our perceptions and thoughts are the reality. It is better to be humble and understand that reality supersedes any model or reports. As such, it is important to gather information and have honest advisors who will inform you of the facts.

The reality may be significantly different from the approved plan. Joe and Jane may be doing other things on those dates. The first reflex is to say that if the project manager is doing his job correctly, that should not happen. Just be a better taskmaster, be a better planner, and there will be no problems during the execution phase of a project. However, life has a way of throwing reality back in our faces. Enough experience will teach you that, despite our carefully formed plans, we can expect things to happen differently. The plan never perfectly survives contact with reality.

This is not to say that plans are not useful. It would be wrong to reach the conclusion that all the planning and various processes involved are not valuable. A good plan is essential for the success of the project, and it is important to invest enough energy into planning activities. However, in a dynamic world, it is equally important to be brutally honest and admit reality as it is. You cannot make the world and the future totally predictable. The future will always include its measure of uncertainties. That is why you need leadership skills in tandem with the expertise and proper use of the various tools and techniques existing in the necessary knowledge areas. You need to understand that all tools, templates, project plans, and documentation are an approximation of reality. It is important to ensure that they remain what they are supposed to be: tools.

The power of reality

We live in a dynamic world with fast-paced changes. New knowledge and innovations are appearing at a faster pace than ever before. The social environment is evolving rapidly. Even the pace of change for laws and policies is different. The speed of change brings a profound impact on how we plan and operate. In a static world, change is the exception and must be managed, and processes can be planned and designed for the long term. In a dynamic world, however, change is the new normal. Change is constant and fast, so it is essential to adapt. Our mind needs to remain alert, open to new learning for us as the leader and for our team members.

A dynamic world requires the development of leadership skills to navigate our constantly changing culture. This dynamic world also brings the need for dynamic analysis, rapid decision-making, and the ability to stay clear on a vision despite numerous unknowns. I like this quote from Søren Kierkegaard, a Danish philosopher of the 19th Century (1813-1855)[15]:

> "There are two ways to be fooled. One is to believe what isn't true. The other is to refuse to accept what is true.[16]"

As the leader of your project, you want to successfully complete the project. To do so, don't be fooled.

---

[15] Wikipedia Søren Kierkegaard
http://en.wikipedia.org/wiki/Søren_Kierkegaard
[16] Quote from Søren Kierkegaard - Quoteswave.com
http://www.quoteswave.com/picture-quotes/408748

CHAPTER 11

Survey on leadership

Introduction

While preparing this book, I created a survey which was distributed to key project managers in my network and on various forums, groups, and communities on the Internet. Among other things, I tried to identify the biggest challenges of project managers.

For the purist in statistics, this survey may not have all the attributes required to be a perfect one. However, for our purpose, it is definitely helpful. It provides interesting insights into the minds of experienced project managers. These people have real experiences and are interested in the subject of leadership in project management. They are seeking to enhance their results through better leadership skills.

Some interesting data on the profile of the respondents: 2/3 were men and 1/3 women. Respondents were distributed fairly equally among age groups.

Less than 30	-	18 %
Age 30 - 39	-	27 %
Age 40 - 49	-	18 %
Age 50 - 59	-	27 %
60 and up	-	10 %

Number of projects managed at the same time:

1 project	-	9 %
2-3 projects	-	46 %
4-6 projects	-	27 %
7 or more	-	18 %

Of course, the above question does not consider the size of the projects. It is easier to manage multiple small projects than many large ones. However, the question does show some level of experience in portfolio management.

Summary of results

Below is a summary of the results of the survey.

Interest in adding leadership skills

- Leadership skills were viewed as a differentiator between a good project manager and an average project manager. The survey identified the following rationale for developing leadership skills:
- Leadership is perceived as a tool to help manage people. At times, the requirements to manage people can be viewed as random, while the mechanics of project management are considered easier than managing people.
- Communication is important for project managers. Leadership skills help provide better communication with the organization and within the team.
- The role of the project manager must include both effective leadership and an understanding of the tools and techniques necessary for effective project management.

- Leadership skills help influence the behaviors, attitudes, and thoughts of all the team members, and align the team toward a similar vision.
- Often, the project manager has limited authority. Leadership skills help to develop and exercise influence on various stakeholders.
- Some believe that the role should be called project leader, rather than project manager, because leadership is an integral part of project management.
- Project managers are there to lead as servant leaders, not to fill up project management templates.
- While there are management aspects to the role of project manager, leadership is the biggest factor in determining success on large projects.

What does leadership in project management mean?

Here is a summary of the answers provided for this question:

- A project leader should be able to provide vision and guidance to the project team, and help them understand the vision and the value the project will deliver.
- Motivating the team. Leadership means bringing the team up from low morale and being the one who wraps things up and closes while everyone else leaves work early.
- Providing guidance and explaining the vision and rationale, not just giving orders on what and how to do the tasks.
- Being able to delegate tasks to people and trust that they will take care of the task and make sure that it is delivered.
- Being able to communicate and lead a team with maximum productivity.

- It's about asking the right questions and being fair in conversation.
- Being able to make strategic and timely decisions.
- Leadership in project management is the ability to set the direction by helping others see what lies ahead and rising to the challenges in a collaborative manner.
- Being an exceptional team leader and always having great relationships with stakeholders.
- Ultimately, a project manager leads by influencing the attitudes, behavior, and decisions of the project team, sponsor, and other stakeholders.

What is your greatest challenge as a project manager?

Here is a summary of the greatest challenges as a project manager identified by the respondents to the survey:

- I continually work on my communication skills. Finding the proper balance between not enough communication and too much of it. It is important to communicate the right information to the appropriate level for each stakeholder.
- Not being able to communicate with some members of the team, the customer, the users, or any stakeholders.
- Communication must be adapted to the character of the people. If the communication fails, the project will fail.
- Keeping my team productive and collaborative without my personal involvement with every task.
- Coordinating teams in a global environment, and defining the constraints and liberties of the work environment.
- Maintaining participation by project team members not 100% assigned to the project, and where their management has not made the project their most important activity.

- Getting stakeholders aligned and engaged in the project and getting everyone to work together to maximize project benefits for everyone concerned.
- The greatest challenge is to create the collaborative environment.
- Obtaining a strong support from senior management.
- Being unaware of political motivations of individuals.
- Excessive complexity in the governance structure can cause problems, rendering the timely decision-making process very difficult.
- Complying with processes designed and governed by project theorists, who confuse artifacts such as stage gate documentation with the actual project deliverables.
- Customers coming with a prepared solution and being unable to explain which problem will be solved... In such cases, it is definitely a good example requiring enough leadership and courage to discuss it with the client, for the better good of their project.

Key strengths as a leader

The survey asked project managers what they viewed as their current key strengths as a leader. Here is a summary of the results:

- Being picky and meticulous; "trying to gather all the information I need in one place as much as possible."
- Providing good communication and motivation.
- Being enthusiastic, part of the team, protecting the team and promoting their results.
- Communication, commitment, positive attitude.
- Team leadership, mentoring team members.
- Respect, inspirational, caring, and visionary.
- Long experience gets me credibility, and as long as I can build on that, I tend to be successful.
- My passion and capacity to share a vision and include people in a collaborative journey towards this vision.

- I can maintain a positive attitude in all situations, and critique subordinates without putting them on the spot or damaging their self-esteem.
- Willing to talk and listen to team members.
- Developing a rapport with individuals; allowing each person to have a voice in collaboration.

Main challenges and weaknesses in being an effective leader

The survey asked project managers what they viewed as their current main challenges and weaknesses in being an effective leader. Here is a summary of the results:

- Time management. The major weakness is that I do not trust the team behind me. They can do a sloppy job, and I have to cover up for them.
- Being female makes it harder.
- Sometimes I control too much, more than is necessary.
- Ability to inspire, creativity, intuition.
- Understanding and adapting to the organizational culture.
- Communication is often identified as a challenge.
- I'm always an outsider, and it's easy to be marginalized by some dominant personality who wants to undermine the project, or by the group that brought me in.
- Letting go of one's ego and having the humility to accept that in order to lead, one must depend on others and accept that leadership be distributed. I am easy to satisfy but difficult to please. I need to verbalize my appreciation for task completion more often to subordinates.
- Experienced specialists such as engineers who do not care about any management advice or any newly implemented processes.

- Knowing when I have enough information to make a decision. At some point, you have to decide, but I always wonder if some hidden information would enable a better decision.

The top challenges of projects

The survey tried to identify the top challenges of projects that project managers are facing in their work. Here is the list of the most frequently identified challenges:

- Stakeholder management,
- Effective meetings,
- Ability to make timely and effective decisions,
- Interaction with senior management,
- Delegation,
- Time management,
- Contract management, and
- Understanding politics within an organization.

Conclusion

Many of the topics above are covered in this book, which is designed to provide a global view of project management. The elements included in this toolbox should assist the project manager in developing their leadership skills and achieving better results in a dynamic world. Developing leadership skills is a complex and lifelong journey. It is a journey that is started, but is never fully accomplished. There is no easy formula. It is like learning music. You can become good at it, even a virtuoso, but you can never completely master the art.

The key is to value leadership and the journey to learn and grow as a leader. Being interested in the subject and taking action to become a better leader is ultimately the most important step to achieve better results.

CHAPTER 12

Keys to project success

The most important thing

This is an often-asked question: "What is the most important thing in project management?"

Various answers are available in books, articles, and forums. They cover a broad range of options and are often tied to the specialization of the author. The person who sells communication expertise will talk about communication, while another person specializing in human resources and team management programs will talk about team management, and another may focus on stakeholder engagement. The planner will simplify everything as a planning issue.

It is like the famous saying: If you have a hammer, everything will look like a nail. In the end, these experts are all talking about processes and tools, but a project does not fundamentally exist to give life to processes and tools. Let's return to the basics.

What are the keys to being a successful project manager?

To succeed, a project manager must focus on the three key concepts:

- Results,
- Decisions, and
- Actions.

Everything else is designed to optimize the management of the project, which is obviously important. You do want to be an efficient project manager. However, it is impossible to be a successful project leader without mastering these three keys to project success.

Results

At the core, a project is trying to accomplish something, a defined result. To be effective as a project leader, the required tasks must be completed successfully. There is no way around it. As such, it is imperative to clearly identify the intended results of the project. This is why the planning phase is so important.

Throughout the life of the project, the intended result has to remain present in our mind. It will be at the center of everything: planning, assigning tasks, monitoring, quality control, and obtaining client approval. Project management methodology, tools, and processes exist to help the project team succeed. They provide a full toolbox, but the intended results give the direction.

It is fundamental to always keep your eyes fixed on the intended results. Otherwise, project management methodology may start to have a life of its own. It can begin to exist for its own benefits, or just for academic or compliance purposes. Without a focus on results, the project runs the risk of just playing with project management tools and not delivering any added value at the end.

This is a frequent cause of troubled or failed projects: The project team lost sight of the intended results. To rescue such projects, an essential first step is to realign everybody on the objective of the project. This may also include recalibrating the governance structure and methodology.

Decisions

No project can be successful in the absence of strong and timely decisions. From the very beginning of the project, numerous decisions must be made to achieve the final objective. Otherwise, this objective will stay just a dream or a wish.

A project leader must be skillful at making decisions. He must also be good at obtaining decisions from others when required. This is fundamental; otherwise, the lack of decisions will kill any chance of success. Decisions will be required throughout the whole life of the project. Unless it is a very simple and very predictable one, it is impossible to design a plan and execute it without making subsequent decisions. Such is real life; reality is far too complex.

Timely decision-making, easy or hard, is a core requirement for project success. This applies not only to the project manager, but also to the governance structure of a project. The setup of the governance structure can create issues, delays, and failure to meet performance targets, even for simple projects.

A project led by a project manager unable to make decisions can easily fail. To be a leader, a project manager must be more than a Taskmaster. A project manager must demonstrate leadership skills and the ability to make good and timely decisions. His ability will have a substantial impact on the success of the project, and also on the trust and relationship he has with the project team, the sponsor, and other stakeholders.

Actions

Finally, you need actions. The optimal project manager must be action-oriented. Otherwise, the project becomes a theoretical exercise. Even if it complies with the standards, which is great in the academic world, it falls short in day-to-day life.

In the real world, the project manager cannot escape this reality: no action, no results. It is that simple. Project management is very results-driven.

As Peter Drucker (1909 - 2005[17]) said:

> "Plans are only good intentions unless they immediately degenerate into hard work.[18]"

Leadership is more than words. You can only go only so far with good thoughts and motivational speeches. You need actions. Over the long term, the reputation of a leader will be based on his ability to take action and achieve results.

Project success

If a project manager focuses on the intended results, makes decisions, and takes constant action during the project, he will have a far greater chance of succeeding.

Throughout all phases of the project, a good project manager should be focused on the objective. He will have to ensure that actions are taken, monitor the projects, and make timely decisions to achieve the objective.

In being strategic and focusing on the objective, it is also important to consider the full impact of the project. This is

---

[17] Wikipedia - Peter Drucker
http://en.wikipedia.org/wiki/Peter_Drucker
[18] Quote from Peter Drucker on Quoteswave.com
http://www.quoteswave.com/text-quotes/16513

even more important in a dynamic world, characterized by fast changes in knowledge, technology, business, and the social environment. Beyond the specific benefit of a project, it may bring other benefits. A strategic leader will know how to connect the dots and communicate this larger vision to stakeholders.

Did the project fuel another initiative with some of its components, innovations, and lessons learned? Did it morph into something even more useful? It may have successfully delivered something of equal or even higher benefits to the organization. In such cases, the changes should be welcomed and gladly integrated into the project. In some contexts, insisting on delivering the initial version of the plan will result in a perfect project delivering a weaker product.

The strategic role of the project leader is to be able to connect the dots and have a larger vision than the project, to be able to see its integration with other process, components, etc. To become a successful leader, the project manager should ultimately raise his thinking to this global, strategic level.

CHAPTER 13

Strategic view of planning

Introduction

In this chapter, we will present an overview of some strategic items to consider in planning. This is neither a guidebook on planning nor a full course on the subject. Other books happen to fill that duty and should already have been studied by the project manager. These other books may, however, be very tactical. Our focus here is on the strategic role to be played as an effective leader.

What are the strategic considerations to address as a leader during planning? This chapter focuses on this dimension of planning.

Defining the result

Defining the expected results is a critical part of project management. If you don't know where you are going, your path can lead you anywhere. You must define where you are going and then find the right path to get there. Project management provides a comprehensive approach, including tools and techniques, to help provide such a successful completion.

Ultimately, project success must be measured by the ability to execute and deliver the intended results. There may be a desire in the beginning to rush and start to work right away on the project, but it is crucial to slow down and plan the project phases properly.

Project managers are often concerned about scope creep, an unauthorized expansion of the scope of the project, resulting in increased cost, delayed timelines, or reduced quality. Documenting the project requirements is a fundamental activity. Scope creep, if not well managed, can be very dangerous for a project.

The planning phase will put in place the foundation of success for a project by documenting the project objective and scope and its requirements. The first step is understanding the project requirements, which are the usual technical specifications of the project.

Understanding the why?

The task of defining results should be more strategic than just documenting the objective and scope and then using this as a method to control tasks, work packages, and changes.

To bring leadership skills to the project and enhance the value of the project for the client, it is essential to understand more than managing scope. A strategic player tries first to perceive clearly and understand the rationale behind the project. This is the *"why"* behind the business case.

- Why are we doing this project?
- What problem are we trying to solve?
- What opportunities are we trying to exploit?

This requires a strategic discussion with senior management and other key stakeholders early in the life of the project. What is their vision about it? What do they need at the end of this project? Why do they care about this project?

Remember that a senior executive will assume you will use the proper skills and methodology, but that is not what they focus on. There is something that they want out of this project. It may be obvious from the project description and initial discussion, or it may not.

As a leader, don't take it for granted that the *why* will be clearly communicated. It is risky in leadership to make assumptions, so don't assume that the information provided during the project initiation is exact, complete, and the best solution.

Defining the rationale behind the project also provides support for strategic decision-making throughout its lifetime. During the planning phase of a project, it is important to gather a holistic view of the project by understanding the rationale and the problem it is trying to solve or the opportunity it is trying to exploit.

Understanding stakeholders

Often, you have other key stakeholders to consider. They can be other units in the organization, users, or external stakeholders. You must understand their point of view. This is important, not just an external, optional consideration. The inability to grasp their point of view can become a key cause of failure after the project is completed, even if it meets all the project requirements.

Leadership requires the project manager to step back and connect the dots. He must be able to see the connections between the project and other processes, threats, opportunities, initiatives, and so on.

Assessing your project

Project management is such a diverse world that advice relevant for one kind of project may be dangerous for another type, so it is essential to assess correctly what type of project you are managing. The choice of approach, methodology, tools, techniques, and competency required for team members will have to be adjusted to your current project.

Projects vary in nature, and it is our job as leaders to understand the kind of project we are managing. This section presents some key characteristics of a project which will impact the choice of methodology.

Duration

The duration of the project will have an impact on the project methodology you use. For example, a longer duration will require more project status reports, stakeholder engagements, and monitoring of progress. Short duration projects are more *"go and do."*

Complexity

Complexity is a key element to assess at the earliest time possible. High complexity projects must be managed very differently than simple, task-based projects. Complexity increases the unknown and potential risks in the project.

Uniqueness of the project

A project that is one of a kind, unique, and new is harder to manage. You do not benefit from past experience, and you are deprived of lessons learned from previous projects. A new, unique project will include more assumptions and less proven information to build the project plan, and it will require more intense monitoring.

Size of the project team

The size of the team will have a huge impact on the project methodology. A project team created to build a bridge will not be the same as a five-person team formed to organize a conference. A huge, epic project will need a project management team with assistants helping to delegate tasks, update documents, monitor tasks, facilitate meetings, and produce reports. For these projects, the project manager is not doing any work on the tasks, but is fully occupied by management and coordination activities. Based on those projects with a sufficiently large size, you will often hear advice that the project manager should delegate, ensure all the appropriate work packages are done, and not do any work on the tasks themselves.

While this approach is appropriate for large projects, it would not work on small ones. If you have a smaller project, such an approach will make the project manager a burden, an overhead cost, not adding any value.

Design and creativity

A project based on known and predictable tasks is different from a project that has a design and creativity component. Too often, design and creativity projects are planned and managed as if you can order creativity. For example, facilitating ten meetings in a two-week period works with predictable tasks and work effort requirements. However, creativity is more fluid and more subject to trial and error, building, doing, undoing, moving forward, and moving backward until you have the best version.

Integration

Some projects are fully completed by one team, in which all members interact with one another regularly. Other projects have various components assigned to different resources, internal or external (contractors), located in different buildings, cities, or even countries. If these people work for different organizations, they also have different interests, constraints, and orders which they must deal with. The latter will require a project manager to perform the integration of all the components of the projects, whereas integration is not an issue with the first example.

It is essential to understand the different levels of requirement. If a person is used to being in a project requiring precise monitoring by the project manager to integrate the various components, and then moves to a project with low-integration requirements, he will have to adjust to the lesser complexity of the new project. Otherwise, imposing the same role on the project manager will become a useless overhead cost, not a value-added activity.

So the key question is, *"Did you assess your project and its level of complexity?"* Many other decisions will change based on the answer to this question.

The choice of methodology

It is a tricky question, which proper methodology to use.

Why? By definition, every project is different. Project management does not exist in overthinking or overanalyzing. It is about delivering a result, and that result is the ultimate measure of success. This is the guideline for the selection of methodology: select the right tools and techniques to achieve success in the most effective and efficient manner.

It is not wise to blindly apply all the concepts in project management to all projects. The context of the project should be considered, and the methodology adapted to it. If you indiscriminately apply all the best practices in business management to an organization, you will kill that organization. A practice is only *the best* given the context and circumstances.

Project management methodology doesn't need to be complicated or torturous. Each project has its own level of complexity, and the choice of methodology must be aligned accordingly. This is the fundamental strategic decision a leader must make as project manager. Project complexity is already a challenge of its own. If a project is simple, then you will kill a project by loading the burden of excessive methodology on it. If a project is complex, then you will let it collapse by using insufficient methodology.

We must regret that some project managers don't care enough about the results they are supposed to achieve. They become methodologists: preaching for their system, maybe a customized system they are selling, maybe even a great idea they had in the past that worked well twenty years ago in a certain context. They forget that it worked in a different era, in a very specific context. They become methodologists.

Process can take over and obscure the work to be done. Then it becomes a dragon, a big overhead that increases the cost and reduces the value for the client. The process can become a huge tax on the project, instead of an enabler. Each project is unique, and the methodology used should add value, not be an overhead luxury cost, and should support achieving the intended results.

We are not process cops. We are in the service of delivering project for others. We are servant leaders, not enforcers of a methodology. The key performance indicator is when senior people in the organization and clients start to see us as adding value, rather than just a high overhead required as per some book.

For large projects, structure is everything, from stakeholder engagement minutes to work trackers and custom reports. People managing projects of high complexity and large size will use formal methodologies. For smaller projects, formalized approaches may be superfluous, but an organized and structured report with quality templates will be extremely useful.

One of the big decisions that a project manager must make is deciding which processes and tools to implement. PMBOK is a massive guide, designed to cover all potential projects. Projects can be small, medium, or large, lasting for a few weeks, months, or even a few years, such as when building a bridge.

> "The acceptance of project management as a profession indicates that the application of knowledge, processes, skills, tools, and techniques can have a significant impact on project success. The PMBOK Guide identifies that subset of project management body of knowledge that is generally recognized as good practice. 'Generally recognized' means the knowledge and practices described are applicable to most projects most of the time, and there is consensus about their value and usefulness. 'Good practice' means there is general agreement that the application of the knowledge, skills, tools, and techniques can enhance the chances of success over many projects. 'Good practice' does not mean that the knowledge described should always be applied uniformly to all projects; the organization and/or project management team is responsible for determining what is appropriate for any given project.[19]"

It may be tempting to say, *"It's in PMBOK, so let's use it,"* or to apply the same formula to all projects. However, this will not be the best approach to achieve the intended results of the project. Even worse, a bad strategic decision on how to deliver the project may be the cause of numerous problems and even the cause of failure of the project.

This is a strategic and fundamental mistake. This is project management at the robotic level, removing any leadership and decision-making and value-added from the role of the

---

[19] How to use PMBOK, PMBOK, p. 2

project manager. We must remember that everything depends on the project characteristics and level of complexity.

Assembling the project team

Once you have a good understanding of the project requirements and the complexity of the project, the most critical step is assembling the project team. A good plan delivered by a weak team will always be a weak proposition.

The project team should be built to maximize collaboration and competency as a whole. It is essential to have the proper diversification of skills, rather than hiring employees or contractors who all have the same skills.

Skills are important, but a project is more like a team sport than an individual sport. The success of the team will depend on its ability to collaborate, share ideas, and learn from others. Effective collaboration maximizes the strength of the product and the group as a whole. On the other hand, ineffective teams tend to have conflicts and individualized views. There is less creativity, collaboration, and learning between team members.

Know your team. Be sensible about your own and their capabilities.

Conclusion

Strategic thinking is an important contribution of a project leader. During the planning phase, a leader must go beyond the mechanical aspect of the methodology. Still, it is important to correctly define the scope of the project and the deliverables. It is also important to invest proper time in defining and budgeting how the work will be completed.

A strategic view of the planning process will make sure the project manager has a full understanding of the rationale behind the project. He will also invest sufficient time in understanding the complexity of the project. This information will guide him and the project team in selecting the most appropriate methodology to deliver value to the client. The planning phase is also a critical period to align all stakeholders and ensure a common understanding of the project.

Strategic thinking is required to be a leader and manage a project at a higher level than simple planning and supervision of tasks.

CHAPTER 14

Managing the project

Introduction

I believe the most overlooked part of PMBOK is the execution phase, along with monitoring and control. In the end, we are doing a project to accomplish something, and it is in the execution phase that this happens. Without proper execution, the idea remains an idea, a concept. Successful entrepreneurs don't have better ideas than others, but they do excel at execution. They are action-oriented, and because of that, they are ahead of the game. In a dynamic world, they have completed all tasks and are *"live"* when others are still thinking and doing analysis.

A strategic leader positively serves the project. He doesn't just occupy a comfortable position.

Project execution is fundamental

If we want to produce something, we must have a realistic plan. Then, even more importantly, there is project execution, which is about making sure the plan is delivered. A leader must be action-oriented and focused on results. A project can have a very detailed and thorough plan and still deliver nothing if project execution fails.

We should be measured by the results we accomplish, not by the quantities of project management templates we can stack within a period of time. Project management is all about delivering results. The tools that we use should support us in achieving this objective, rather than the other way around. A good project is well supported by methodology, tools and processes. A good selection of these will ease the work of the project team and assist them in completing the various tasks.

Unfortunately, we can sometimes feel that the opposite is the case, that the project team must adapt the project to the methodology, tools, and processes.

Ideas without execution will remain dreams—beautiful dreams, but still just dreams. Plans without execution are academic exercises, enjoyable for the mind, but that's it. As a strategic leader, you are mandated to deliver, and you will be measured on your ability to deliver. That is all done in the execution phase. Your ability to lead the project and show real results is the ultimate performance indicator.

A good plan will help you deliver efficiently, but a plan on its own will do nothing. At some point, someone has to deliver on the plan.

Project Information Management

Managing project documents is essential in a project if you want to complete tasks and monitor and control the project efficiently. It is even more important in professional services and knowledge areas. I have seen too many projects in which the digital information was just dumped on a shared drive. Changing a team member during the project becomes very complicated when this happens, because there is no logical way to find the information.

In contrast, if information is sufficiently structured and the project is using project management, team collaboration, and communication tools, then when someone is sick or on vacation, it is easy for others to continue the work and find the relevant information.

It may feel that a solid project information management system is not a strategic issue for a leader. But it is. The system will either be a constant constraint or an enabler during the life of the project. As a leader, it is important to pay attention to this element of the project.

Project documents

A project can generate a stack of documents. Among others, you can find the following key documents in physical cabinets, but most often in digital format: project charter, business cases, project plan, requirements, stakeholder register, risk register, and project status reports.

The list can include many more items, all the way to the lessons learned at the end of the project. Some kinds of projects, such as business consulting and advisory, tend to create documents as deliverables, based on an analysis of other documents and the results of analytical working papers.

Information management happens to be only lightly discussed in project methodology. Project management methodologies mostly discuss tools, techniques, and processes that generate documents. For many processes, it is considered a best approach, if not a required approach, to document the various parts of managing a project. However, it is often assumed that either a system exists to organize these documents, or somehow project team members will just make it work.

It is important to organize project information in an efficient way. Team members should use the same structure and share the same awareness of the location of information. I love digital life and a paperless process, but I must admit that sometimes the paper world would more automatically force documents to be organized. The project files would be put in binders, and they would be stored in a particular cabinet.

The digital world makes it very easy to create, edit, and share documents. Unfortunately, the contents of a shared drive are also less visible. Often in organizations, you don't even see the servers. The result can easily be that the electronic documents are mismanaged. Documents are just dumped on the hard drive and become useless over time. Too many documents are kept, making it difficult to find the one you are looking for and creating confusion between team members.

Poor project information management will cause huge inefficiency and often negatively impact the quality of the final deliverables. It is the responsibility of the project manager and the project team to make sure the information is indeed there.

Digital context

Nowadays, the work environment is often mostly, if not solely, digital. In the past, a paper binder of documents would have been maintained, but in 2015, it is much more common to have all project documents managed electronically on a hard drive. I personally love being paperless and am all set up in my personal life to work with only electronic documents. It all started a few years ago when my printer broke and I didn't replace it. The lack of a printer forced me to organize myself to work with just the electronic documents. Nothing beats having no other option to force us to adapt and find solutions.

Having good information management for electronic documents is doable, but it requires a system. That is no different from dealing with a paper-based system. However, based on my experience, the digital world makes it easy to hide chaos. In a paper-based system, if the documents are unorganized, the binder is jumbled and documents are floating all over the place in the office. The visibility of the chaos often creates a good pressure to organize. In order to organize the office, a system is then created. The simple act of creating a physical binder often forces us to create a structure for the project information.

In the digital world also, a structure for storing information is necessary, just like one used for physical documents. However, because the chaos on a hard drive is less visible, I have witnessed many projects with very bad information management. Too often, the hard drive (or shared drive, or even cloud storage) becomes a dumping ground for all documents. As such, the project information in the digital world can suffer from the following problems:

- Too many versions of documents,
- Documents obtained but not required for the project,
- Missing key documents,
- Unstructured storage of documents,
- Difficulty in locating proper documents,
- Structure too complex,
- Structure only understood by one or two persons,
- Numerous storage places, or
- Each team member dumping documents only on their private hard drive.

Fixing the information management system is frequently high on the list of elements to repair when rescuing a project.

Tips and advice on information management

The subject may not be discussed often, but it is important to have a good information management system for our project. It is important to ensure that proper documentation exists, can be managed efficiently, and can easily be found in the future. Organization is very important to manage and efficiently deliver the project. Without it, every request for information or project performance reports will take far too much time to accomplish. You want to spend your time completing deliverables, not searching for documents.

Regretfully, I must say that every project in trouble that I have helped has had this common problem. The hard drive is always an information dump, as disorganized as can be. Even if the project is following a good methodology, too often those methodologies assume that there is a process or a system to manage documents. This is a big assumption, and often an inaccurate one, although it may be true if you work in a large organization with an enterprise-level system. Without a system to manage project information, the percentage of time spent looking for documents, searching for information, and preparing performance reports is increased significantly.

Below are some tips and advice to manage project information.

Structure: Establish with the team a structure from the beginning of the project that will be used by all team members, including you. Avoid the mistake of lazily dumping documents on a drive.

Common drive: No information should be stored on private drives. Otherwise, just one employee out sick or on vacation becomes a problem for the rest of the team.

Simplicity: Do not make the structure too complex. If the structure involves too many folders and sub-folders, it becomes very difficult to decide where a document should go, and retrieving it will become an overwhelming challenge.

Ease of understanding: Make the structure easy to understand, not just for the project manager, but for the whole project team. Ideally, it should be reasonably easy to understand for new team members, or for future reference. Don't use cryptic labels.

Keep it clean: Transition copies should be deleted. Often to protect ourselves, we create temporary working versions of documents. It is useful to have them in case of failure or just a need to start fresh from a previous version. However, these needs are temporary, and the transition versions should be deleted. It is useless and confusing to have 32 working versions of a report.

eLibrary: The structure should simplify saving documents that may be useful in many other project areas. A nice approach is to create a project document eLibrary for those documents and refer to them as needed. With this approach, the global documents are only saved once.

Document inbox: To avoid chaos, if there are documents that you are unsure of where to save them, create an inbox for documents on the drive to create a place for them temporarily until you can process and organize them.

Key emails: Include important emails in the project information system by saving them as PDFs. Emails that stay in the user email app tend to be disconnected from the project and impossible for other team members to access. This is why I also love cloud project management and team collaboration apps.

Transparency: Be as transparent as possible with project information. Sometimes I find that chaos helps people hide information, and I do believe that being transparent and honest in communication is a key success factor.

Finally, as part of project closing, it is important to do a periodic review of the project information and clean and reorganize it as needed.

Risk management

Risk management is essential to the success of a project. The team can spend as much time as they want in creating a detailed project plan, but things will not always happen as planned. Some even claim that the project plan will never survive contact with reality. Just like a map, a project plan will always be a simplification of reality, since not everything about the project is fully known, and not everything can be planned in advance. Uncertainties are part of managing a project. A long-term and complex project in a complex and dynamic environment will even have more uncertainties.

Risk management is a tool to manage uncertainties proactively in order to increase the success of the project. In more detail, risk management means maximizing our ability to minimize threats and seize opportunities during the life of the project.

The first requirement for effective risk management is an awareness of uncertainties; then different risk responses are available. The second requirement is to understand that uncertainties are unavoidable. They are part of project management and cannot all be eliminated through planning. As a leader, it is important to create a work environment that encourages open and honest discussions on the subject. But if a project manager always responds to issues with the statement that more planning should have been done, his attitude will disable the risk management process.

It is also crucial to precisely define and communicate what is meant by risks. I prefer the word *"uncertainties,"* because, in most people's minds, risk is defined as negative only. In textbooks, risk covers both positive and negative events. However, this definition makes conversations difficult. It is odd for most people, except experts in risk management, to use the word risk for positive events. Very few will say something like, *"There is a risk that my children will live a healthy life,"* or, *"There is a risk that my marriage will be successful."*

A comprehensive risk management program should include both threats and opportunities. In this program, it is important to define and communicate the definition of risks. It is a dangerous source of confusion if a project manager assumes that all stakeholders are familiar with the textbook definition of risk. A solution I often use is to call it uncertainties management, since risk management is the management of uncertainties to maximize opportunities and minimize threats during the life of the project.

Different models exist to support risk management, including a qualitative and quantitative assessment of risk. Using numbers provides support and a useful analytical tool. Risks can be analyzed, ranked, and prioritized with quantitative analysis. However, while these numeric values provide support, they are not scientific measures. It is important to be able to interpret them and understand what they mean and do not mean.

Often you will see books discussing how to build a risk analysis model. A simple example may be:

70 % expected result: $100,000
30 % expected return: $ - 25,000
Expected return: $62,500

This calculation is true if you have a portfolio of activities and run the same process sufficient times to have a normal distribution. Otherwise, it is a decision tree. You will be on path A or Path B, not on the average path. Think of it like health. Statistics may say that one person has a probability of having disease A of 0.05%, which is true at the population level. At the individual level, however, you either have the disease or you don't. It is a binary decision tree. You never have only 0.05% of the disease. You have it or you don't. That is because at the individual level, you only have one draw, not a normal distribution.

I love numbers and spreadsheets, which can be built to properly manage a project. However, you have to understand what the numbers mean and what they don't mean. It is easy to be fooled by a spreadsheet that can give you precision at the $0.01 for every calculation, but that does not mean that the calculation is precise. If the input is only general assumptions, then the output is also just a general number.

Identify all scenarios that your organization may sustain, including the downside scenarios and those that would be fatal. If they would be fatal, then you have to make a decision to mitigate them fully, to transfer or avoid the threat.

The strategic value-added part of risk management is obtained in the awareness of risks and the establishment of risk responses. For threats, risk responses include mitigate, accept, transfer, or avoid threats; for opportunities, responses include expect, accept, transfer, or exploit the opportunities. Awareness of uncertainties will increase the potential of success of the project and enhance the benefit it can provide to an organization.

When leading a project, the project manager should be aware and sensitive to uncertainties that can have an impact on the project. The risk management process will enable him, and the project team, to maximize opportunities and minimize threats, which will help make the project successful.

Meetings

Meetings are like a virus, often annoying and unavoidable. They should be useful, but they are often less useful than planned or wished. A leader has the fortunate role of chairing various meetings. As such, he is in a position to avoid the pitfalls of bad, unproductive meetings.

Objective

Understand the goal of the meeting. Identify and communicate what you want to accomplish at the beginning of the meeting. The agenda should make it easy for attendees to understand the purpose of the meeting and prepare accordingly.

Method of communication

There are numerous methods of communication, and meetings are just one of them. They should be used appropriately, and not as the default option. Depending on the objectives, other methods of communication may be more effective and less costly.

Duration

Meetings don't always have to last for exactly an hour, or two hours. If you can do it in 15 minutes, perfect. If you can just walk to someone's office and resolve the issue, great. Often, the amount of time you schedule to accomplish a task is the amount of time it ends up taking. One hour seems to be the default standard, probably based on our electronic calendars. Try scheduling meetings for 30 or 45 minutes, or even just 15 minutes. Saving 15 to 30 minutes here and there adds up. It is important to remember that it is not only your time being taken up, but also the time of all of those attending the meeting. If the meeting is longer than necessary, it is time lost that cannot be used to move the completion of tasks forward.

Attendance

Try to limit meetings to five to seven people if at all possible. When the group becomes larger, the effectiveness of the meeting diminishes rapidly. It becomes an opportunity to comment aimlessly on every topic, and to achieve very little progress on the project.

We should not forget that there is a cost to meetings: the direct cost of all the persons present at the meeting. There is also the opportunity cost of the work not progressing because everybody is occupied with meetings. As such, both the time allocated to meetings and their attendance should be controlled. Often, I wish that we would put a counter at each meeting showing the cost of the meeting, based on the salary of each person attending it.

Strategic discussion

Often, people will listen more than speak in front of someone with authority, so not only it is important to communicate, be transparent and honest, and have two-way communication, but you really have to set the field for a two-way communication. Don't take the few team members who do speak to you for granted. They are the minority. You need to bring everybody on board. You need to create a work environment that will enable everybody to talk. It is your responsibility as a leader to reach out to all, including the team members who tend to speak less.

As such, you need to not only be the leader in team meetings. You also need to learn to alternate between the roles of leader and facilitator. A leader leads; a facilitator is more neutral and is there to ensure that appropriate dialogue happens with everybody, and that an objective is met.

In a difficult meeting, step back and try to understand the point of view of the other persons. Do this until you can explain their position.

Relationship management

A project is more than processes and methodology, documents, scope, requirements, and so on. A project is completed by people, for people, and with the influence of many other persons. It is important to strategically manage relationships from the very beginning of the project and throughout the life of the project.

Don't wait for official meetings to obtain buy-in for your project. Managing relationships and expectations is a fundamental part of project leadership. If you wait for the official meeting, you will have missed the opportunity to develop relationships and trust that will be precious to have in the future. When issues arise, you will be a stranger and will be treated as one. It will then be too late to start to develop a relationship.

Sometimes your job is not to obtain the buy-in or to make decisions. Sometimes you are a facilitator. It is the responsibility of the project manager to make sure the information is visible to the right persons or committee at the right time. You are the facilitator for this, so you must create a strong network of influencers to implement your project agenda.

In developing relationships, trust is important. Your word should mean something; your promise should be binding. A long-term relationship should be more important than short-term gain.

Managing the project Sponsor

What is a sponsor? According to PMBOK,

"A sponsor is the person or group who provides resources and support for the project and is accountable for enabling success. The sponsor may be external or internal to the project manager's organization. From initial conception through project closure, the sponsor promotes the project. This includes serving as spokesperson to higher levels of management to gather support throughout the organization and promoting the benefits the project brings. The sponsor leads the project through the initiating processes until formally authorized, and plays a significant role in the development of the initial scope and charter. For issues that are beyond the control of the project manager, the sponsor serves as an escalation path. The sponsor may also be involved in other important issues such as authorizing changes in scope, phase-end reviews, and go/no-go decisions when risks are particularly high. The sponsor also ensures a smooth transfer of the project's deliverables into the business of the requesting organization after project closure[20]."

A sponsor is responsible for providing support and enabling project success. From start to finish, the project sponsor should be the champion for the project. It is often the project sponsor who identifies alignment or potential conflicts between organizational strategies and project goals and then communicates these to the project manager. The project sponsor provides financial support, organizational support, integration into the organization, and other support as required.

Sometimes we hear that a lack of executive support for a project can be a significant cause for failure. Sometimes there are issues with the competency of the executive sponsor. It is indeed important for executive sponsors of projects to understand their role and contribute strategically to the success of the project. However, it is a

---

[20] Definition of Project Sponsor, PMBOK, p.32

bit hard to believe that sponsors are so often incompetent, disengaged, or not interested in the success of the project. Often, the success of the project directly impacts his annual performance assessment.

I think that too often people have a weak understanding of the workday of executives. The truth is that they are busy, managing and providing strategic vision and oversight to numerous activities. In large organizations, this is more and more true as you ascend to higher levels of the organization.

The project manager, as I have said frequently, is more than a taskmaster. It is critical to understand the perspective of the project sponsor and to be proactive about the relationship. If you have the benefit of an executive sponsor of high rank in the organization, you have to understand that this person is busy and has delegated the responsibility of the project to you as the project manager.

This does not imply that the project sponsor is remote and disinterested in the project, although you may get that feeling if you are passively waiting for his intervention, which will tend to be periodic, or sporadic, rare, and short.

Even as manager of operations in a large organization, it is important to learn to proactively manage your supervisor. This is less important in the early phase of a career, when your supervisor will be actively present to supervise your work. But things will change as you get promotions. On one hand, you will have more responsibilities. This will give you more freedom to create strategies and manage the team as you want. On the other hand, you will also have the benefit or burden of a more distant boss. At first, this can be viewed as a benefit, but it can quickly turn into a burden if you don't develop the skills to manage upward.

Managing upward may sound strange, but it is actually pretty normal and involves things like ensuring that the appropriate discussion happens at the right time, and that the necessary information is visible. This is also a great skill to have when managing horizontally.

Again, this distance is not a lack of interest. Executives often have many responsibilities. Now, of course, this does not excuse executives who are not performing their role as project sponsors! It just means that you have to carry out your role as a project manager fully. I believe that more project leadership and less task management is important as you progress in your career. Your role extends beyond supervisor tasks and receiving direction from the project sponsor.

At the beginning of a career, relationships are mostly managed from top to bottom. As one progresses up the ladder, however, it is increasingly important to learn to manage from bottom to top as well. Yes, this requires more leadership skills. In fact, you may have to make the decisions. After all, you are the project manager. You may need to make decisions, and then ensure they are transparently communicated to the project sponsor. This gives him an opportunity to react if he doesn't agree, and it allows him to be informed. If he says nothing, this is a form of approval. If necessary, you will receive his comments.

Conclusion

Managing a project properly will enhance its success. During this busy period, it is important as a leader to remain focused on the vision of the project. This role will include a balance between managing the project plan and being strategic. Despite the best planning efforts, a project will have to face uncertainties, and the task supervisor will feel frustrated and overwhelmed when reality does not conform to the plan. It is in these moments that we can see leaders rise to the challenge and lead the team through the storm.

Don't be afraid of being a leader. Your team needs one, just like your sponsor does. A proper balance between management and leadership activities will benefit the project and enhance the value provided by the project.

CHAPTER 15

Project Reports

Introduction

During the beginning of the life of the project, the project team is obtaining information and seeking more details on the objective and scope of the project. During the life of the project, the project manager will assign tasks.

In this period, there will come a time when the need for communication will change direction. The project team will need to communicate information to various persons: the project sponsor, governance bodies, and stakeholders.

At some point, various teams will also need to report to the project manager on the status of the work packages. What kind of progress has been accomplished?

Project reports are sometimes viewed as an administrative requirement which can be time consuming. But they can also be used strategically to support the success of the project. Let's look at how leaders can use project reports.

The type of reports

It is important to note that reports don't all fulfill the same purpose. A report can achieve various goals: strategic monitoring of the project, proper engagement of stakeholders, accountability, and support for decision-making. As such, the design of the report should be aligned with its objective. Too often, project reports are only an administrative exercise of completing a template. The goal of the report is forgotten, and the message is diluted by lack of focus or excess information.

There are three types of reports:

Visibility: The objective of this kind of report is to provide visibility of the activity of the project team. This is useful to report on progress.

Performance management: This type informs on key performance indicators of the project.

Decision-making: In this kind of report, it is essential to know what you are trying to achieve in order to come to a decision.

To be effective, it is important to know the answer to this question: *"Why are we making this report? Who is the audience?"* Hopefully, the report should have another purpose other than just creating documents and filling the project files.

Design of the report

It is a too-frequent error: preparing a report without identifying what type of report is needed. This results in presentations to clients, governance bodies, or senior executives that lack focus and fail to achieve any benefits for the project. A project manager may complain that he is not getting the decision that he needs. The recipient of the report may wonder, what does this mean? What does the project manager want? Nothing useful is achieved with a badly designed report.

Design is very important, because a report is a communication tool. If it doesn't communicate the proper message, then it is just a document for the project file. Communication requires knowing three elements: what are you trying to say, who the audience is, and what the best method of communication is.

First, you have to know what the key message is. Why are you communicating? If it is a regular report, what is the message for this report? Second, you should understand the audience and adapt the message to them. A financial report to the CFO will have different information than a progress report to the board. Finally, the choice of the method of communication should not be just out of habit. Some information is well communicated in a presentation, other information in a report or a spreadsheet. Sometimes a group discussion is needed, or just an email will do.

A significant risk in project management is ineffective communication between those involved and those who need to be kept updated on progress. Establish a regular format, frequency, and pattern of communication with the right people. Think about your audience carefully and tailor messages accordingly. Finally, never forget the power of a good telephone call or face-to-face meeting, particularly to discuss issues, swap ideas, or progress in-depth tasks. You can always capture your decisions and actions in an email afterward.

The identification of the message, the needs of the audience, and the selection of the proper tools will help design a report that is useful to the success of the project. As much as possible, the design should be interesting for the receiver of the information. On that note, keep in mind that if it is boring for you, it is likely to be twice as boring for your reader. As a strategic leader of a project, clarity is also very important. Remember: If you are not getting the decision you need to obtain, maybe you are not asking clearly in your report.

A well-designed report will guide the project on its path to success, rather than being just an administrative requirement.

Information system

Ideally, to support the design of the report, a good and efficient information management system exists for your project. In the past, this would have been a binder with all the project information. Today, it consists mostly of electronic documents. Even collaboration with executives, sponsors, stakeholders, clients, and team members is most often done electronically.

To be effective, all the team members should have a common understanding of the approach to managing information. Otherwise, the shared drive can quickly become the equivalent of a dump or a graveyard, where electronic documents are saved, only to become lost and impossible to retrieve (despite modern search technology). With the right tools, providing appropriate information to the various stakeholders should not be a complex task. The project manager should be spared the effort to dig far to find the information.

Modern project management applications are very useful if used and configured correctly. They make the information easily available. These applications also minimize the need for the project manager to interrupt the team in completing their tasks and ask them to provide their status reports.

Open conversation

Beyond the design of the organizational tool, there are humans completing these documents. The quality and usefulness of the information in the report will depend on the leadership style that you bring to your own team. How do you react when the information is not positive, or the best? A project manager can dislike issues so much that he always has a negative reaction when these issues are raised in a report. The first goal of this type of reaction may be to increase performance of the team. However, it will likely bring some unintended consequences.

As a leader, it is important to understand that many will tone down and censor what they say in the presence of someone in authority. As a project manager, you are one of those persons in authority. If you don't work hard to reduce that natural barrier, you will have to live with the fact that most of your team members will censor some information from you. This censorship will reduce the quality of the information you receive. As a result, your decisions will be based on incomplete, or worse, inaccurate, information.

Your ability to be a leader for the project will depend on your leadership skills and the quality of the information you have for decision-making. As such, it is essential to create a culture that rewards open conversations and truthful dialogue on the state of the project.

Information from others

It is a major issue if the team members feel uncomfortable speaking to you. You can only obtain so much information on your own, so your team members are a key source of information. With your behavior, you will either encourage them to speak the truth, massage the truth a bit, or a lot, or hide as much as possible of the truth from you. If the leader demeans others when they identify a problem, saying that it is their fault, and anyway, they are paid to fix (or prevent) problems, team members will hide the information, hoping to be able to fix it before anyone notices.

The result is biased information, which also means unreliable information. This will have a very negative impact on the ability of the leader to make good decisions.

As a leader, you cannot make quick, good decisions if you have a distorted view of the world. Team members will provide biased information to stay safe, because the leader is often invested with power, and people don't want to suffer bad reactions and emotions from their boss.

The leader must create a positive work environment that is safe for people to speak up, where constructive discussions on issues and sensitive topics can be held and have their place to support the success of the project. The leader should facilitate these discussions, as they will have a positive contribution to the project.

It is also important to encourage your team members to speak their minds on analysis and strategies. Obtaining the varying points of view of many people with different backgrounds and perspectives will enhance the quality of the report and the decisions made. A leader that focuses only on data obtained from persons having the same background and skills as him will have blind spots caused by groupthink.

Leaders should not underestimate how much they contribute to this behavior. The larger your team, the more distance there will be between the operations and you as the leader. The leader should value all information provided by team members, as it will enhance decision-making.

Imagine the consequences if three team members are considering if they should disclose gaps they see in the project plan, or in the execution of the project plan. Their silence may have a critical impact on the success of the project.

Obtaining clean reports may make nice reports, but it doesn't help decision-making. As such, a badly designed report can be the blind spot of the manager and a risk to the project.

Information overload

To improve decision making, you need the right information. Today it is very easy to be buried under large amounts of data and suffer from information overload. We have numerous shared drives full of data, and it is easy at a very low cost to add even more. Spreadsheets can be designed to hold massive amounts of information. There is an easy temptation to create detailed, expert reports in a small font to convince others that you are in control of everything.

In today's world, we do not suffer from a lack of information. We can be in a meeting and do a search on the Internet to find the information we need. On one hand, we have an excessive appetite for small bits of information. The art of doing comprehensive research is a bit lost, unfortunately. Sometimes this is sad, because strategic decisions are often made without proper consideration for the details. On the other hand, we have lots of data. We have databases of information at a level never dreamed of before.

Too much information can be just the same as not enough information, even if it brings the smell of expertise. After all, if someone has so much data, he must be in control of his project. However, even though I love data and spreadsheets, I must admit this: It is easy to be fooled by numbers.

Useful information

To be useful, a report should guide its audience and help them correctly understand the context of the information provided. Strategic analysis of data included in the report will also improve the success of the communication, as it will bring out the message and create a useful discussion.

A good report will provide timely and adequate information to support decision-making. Unless you are managing a very simple project, decision-making will be a regular part of the role of the project manager, in addition to simply managing tasks. Making decisions requires judgment, sometimes courage, and also accurate and timely information. With modern technology and the rapid pace of change in the world, information should be organized and easily accessible.

Conclusion

In the end, remember that your decisions are only as good as the information you have. You may be wise, knowledgeable, and experienced, but if your information data about your current project is weak, it will provide poor support for decision making. Even worse, your experience can actually color your decisions. Without thinking much about it, your mind can fill in the gaps with pieces of information from other sources. This creates a partial representation of reality.

A report can often be just an administrative requirement to comply with the methodology, client requirements, or governance body requests. A much better report supports the project by providing timely information to others to obtain their support, maintain trust, and ensure that the critical decisions are made.

CHAPTER 16

Decision Making

Beyond mastering tasks

There is no way to successfully manage a project without decision-making. At all phases of the project, decisions will be required. While managing a project, never take for granted that an existing problem will, astonishingly, be solved by itself if nobody takes care of it.

During the planning phase, decisions on objective, scope, changes, methodology, or the project plan are made. However, despite the best efforts to plan, a project will rarely be on cruise control during the execution phase. Decisions will be required on issues, resource allocation, and all the various unknowns that will occur during the life of the project.

To be an effective strategic leader for a project, it is important to understand the importance of decision-making. A leader who is only able to motivate his team and build relationships but is not able to correctly manage decisions would quickly develop the reputation of being weak and ineffective when he is needed the most.

Decision-making is not discussed enough in project management. Too often, everything is reduced to predictable tasks, which can be automated. The role of the project manager is then unfortunately reduced to being a taskmaster rather than a project leader. The project manager should be doing more than mailbox management; that is, more than just sending and receiving tasks and documents.

The value-added part of being a strategic project leader includes the ability to make decisions. That is the focus of this chapter: decisions in project management. It is a very important topic, as too many projects in trouble are stuck because decisions are not made.

Making decisions

I once heard a guest say on a podcast, *"Making decisions— excuse me, I mean recommending a decision."* This statement implies that a project manager is not paid to make decisions. However, I have never seen a project in which the project manager was not actually paid to manage and make decisions. If this is the case, then his role has been reduced to task supervisor. Sure, there are boundaries to and around his power. He must respect his mandate, the governance structure of the project, the organization, and ultimately the clients who is paying. After all, unless you are doing a project for yourself, in which case you are the client, some final decisions are left to others.

However, I have never seen a project in which the project manager did not have any authority to decide. If he needs to go to the project sponsor, or to the client, for every decision, then it means that person is now the project manager. Which begs the question: why do we have two project managers on a project, only because the one appointed to the job does not make decisions? That is an overhead cost that doesn't add any value.

It may feel easier to reduce the role of the project manager to being a taskmaster, the person supervising the proper execution of the tasks in the project plan. However, project management benefits from a higher view of the role of project manager: a strategic project leader achieving success and delivering value to clients.

Yes, if you make decisions, you are also accountable. You will bear the burden of the results of your decisions. If you generally make good decisions, you gain a great reputation as someone who can make things happen. If you make bad decisions, others will trust you less, start to watch you more, monitor your project, and control your activities (if not simply reduce them).

If you are not clear on which decisions you can make, discuss this with your clients and sponsor. Discuss the matter with self-confidence and self-awareness. Be aware of what you can do well and what is beyond your expertise.

If you lack expertise in the subject of the project, then, of course, making decisions will be difficult. This is why you must be a project manager only in a field that you can understand. Otherwise, your role is going to be very generic with vague advice, only managing what matters least. As a leader, your strategic contribution to the success of the project will be limited.

When making decisions, it is important to understand the relative importance of the matter. How often have I seen people trying to manage every decision as if the result will be equivalent to the explosion of a nuclear plant! Most decisions are deprived of such grave short- and long-term consequences. It is not a good sign of leadership to constantly request that others make decisions for all the minor issues in a project. Your team needs you to make decisions in a timely manner.

You need to make decisions throughout the life of a project, even if you have a plan. Otherwise, the project manager can be like one who would fly a plane into the side of a mountain because the plan said that was the route to take. In this kind of logic, the plan becomes the reality. But any plan is only an abstraction, a huge simplification of reality, just as a map is a useful but still simplified representation of the reality. During the life of the project, it is important to monitor and adjust the plan. This requires factual information and the ability to make decisions.

Is the project manager the right person to make decisions? For many decisions, yes. Otherwise, he is no more than a task supervisor, adding minimal value. If a project manager sits in his office and is unable to make good decisions for the project, he is just an overhead cost. A lack of timely decisions is often a cause of project failure, so the project should not be led by an indecisive manager.

The decision of others

The art of decision-making is part of being a leader. This doesn't insinuate that you have to be a dictator, making all decisions and imposing your will on everybody else. Yet a leader will ensure that decisions on key issues are made in a timely fashion. The method of making a decision will be adjusted and adapted to the context; there is no one perfect approach. The decisions may also be made by the project team, the project sponsor, the governance structure, the client, or other stakeholders—but decisions will be made.

Once you have made all the decisions you can on your own, there will still be decisions that others have to make. In that case, you have to understand that it is your role to ensure that action is taken, because you as a project manager are able to raise issues to the project sponsor, the governance structure, or the client.

To be effective, you have to make these people aware of the decision and allow them to make it, or at least be aware of the consequences if they don't (transparency and honesty). The way in which we communicate the information and the need for a decision will have an impact on our success in obtaining such decisions. The first requirement is to be clear and direct. Don't use jargon or unanalyzed reports, which list all the things that happened on the project. Say what matters, supported by a clear analysis. Explain the situation clearly to the other person.

Be focused on the results, not the task. Focus on solutions, not on delegating the problem. If you don't have a complete solution and need to consult the sponsor, then present your partial analysis, not just the problem, and the issue that makes you hesitate.

If you are seeking a decision, it is essential to be direct and clear in your request. It is also important to properly understand the context of the other person. If they are busy and cannot meet you until Thursday, it is not due to a lack of interest; it is simply that they are busy handling other matters. Don't be selfish, insensitive, or judgmental.

If the person only has limited time, do not wait for the next time he can afford two hours with you so that you can explain everything. This is not an audit; this is a meeting to obtain strategic decisions for the success of your project. Often you can get much work done with reduced length meetings. How about a 30-minute meeting? 15 minutes? 5 minutes? The famous *"Do you have two minutes?"* should be in your mind.

Even if the decisions must be made by someone else, or by a governing body, it is still possible to influence the process to increase the odds of obtaining this critical decision. That is being a strategic project leader.

Human and difficult decisions

When you are facing difficult decisions, it is important to provide enough space in our minds for awareness of our emotions. Most would agree that it is essential to make sure we don't act on an emotional response. However, it is impossible to avoid this if we are unaware of our emotions.

We are all human beings, and that includes having emotions. Some may pretend that they act solely on rational thinking and have no emotions, but this is a naive approach at best. Emotions exist in some way or another in all of us. That is true even for leaders.

The classic advice of *"sleep on it"* remains a very good idea. If you do not have the time to sleep on a decision, even a simple twenty-minute break can help. Even better, take time to pause and reflect and increase self-awareness through a twenty-minute meditation. This will bring mental clarity that will enhance the critical decision-making process.

Also let others communicate their emotions, in a constructive way, of course, and as the leader, redirect this energy toward solutions. Don't just deny the existence of emotions and pretend that everything is just logic and business. On the other hand, don't fall in the trap of producing only emotional reactions. Collect data and analyze options before making a decision.

We are talking here about negative emotions and issues, but the same concepts would apply equally to positive emotions. Sometimes we may see opportunities and be too quick to jump ahead. Give yourself time to gather facts, assess strategies, and test the reality of implementation. Don't just react on your first impression. Problems will appear, and you can only address them if you admit them, pure and simple. Reality won't change based on our denials of it.

With sufficient self-awareness of ourselves and others, it will be much easier to be a leader, obtain the required facts and analysis, and support the decision-making process.

Courage

Of course, as we discussed earlier in this book, making decisions requires leadership. When you make a decision, you must assume the responsibility of the decision and become accountable for the results. The art of decision-making becomes even more of a challenge when facing difficult decisions, which require courage. As such, it may feel easier to let others make the decisions. That is often the key reason a project manager wants somebody else to make the decision. It has nothing to do with the roles of the project manager, sponsor, and client. It has to do with courage and accountability.

A strategic project leader must have the courage to face issues and make decisions. Being the leader seems like a fun position, since you are the boss. Maybe it was a career dream. Sometimes the position may have some benefits, like meeting senior people in organizations or participating in special meetings and conferences.

But as a leader, you also have to deliver results. At times this will be relatively easy. The strategy is a consensus, and there are very few negative stakeholders, no issues, and no problems. Managing the project is a smooth execution. All you have to do is manage and collect your success.

But more often than not, there will be difficult meetings, disagreements on strategy, difficult employees or stakeholders, and incomplete information to make decisions. It is in these moments that a leader will be challenged the most as a person.

During these moments, courage will become a key component of leadership. As project manager, you will have to raise your game and demonstrate bravery. This is often what separates success and failure in difficult situations. A person with sufficient courage will be able to lead the team, while a person without courage will fail at leading the project.

Without courage, the project manager can fall into many traps:

Analysis paralysis: failing to make a decision because of incomplete information and continuously asking for more analysis;

Lack of communication: failing to communicate accurate information in a timely manner to the right person, for fear of their reaction;

Weak team management: failure to communicate performance information to team members, for fear of their reaction;

Contract management: failure to manage contract performance from a supplier, for fear of their reaction; or

Decision-making: failure to make the appropriate decisions, because it would lead to an emotionally difficult path.

When thinking about courage, I always have in mind the image of an old ship's captain at sea, calmly and wisely leading his crew. The old captain is making decisions with a sense of calm serenity and peace of mind.

Courage is a key component of leadership. If you feel your courage is weakening, it is best to take a break. Seek advice from friends, mentors, the project sponsor, your second-in-command, and your team members.

Presentation to senior management

As a project manager, it is our role to ensure that the appropriate discussions take place at the right time, and that information is visible. This is also a great skill to have when managing horizontally, and it becomes ever more important as you deal with more senior persons in the organization.

Successful project management includes actively managing relationships and stakeholders, including the project sponsor. This is project leadership, not just being a taskmaster.

The project sponsor provides an additional source of expertise that is available during the lifetime of the project, and the manager should strategically consult the project sponsor as required during the whole process. To knock on the project sponsor's door and consult him will often be a necessity for the project manager.

I would say that the problem is larger than project management. Too often, presentations given at senior executive meetings lack focus. They are written to provide a lot of general information, but they fail to answer the question, what do you need from me (us, if a governance body)? When preparing a presentation, it is essential for success to identify what you are trying to achieve, and then aim for it.

Conclusion

The ability to make decisions is an essential part of leadership. It is also something that will help you as a strategic project leader obtain trust from everybody: your team members, the sponsors, and stakeholders.

The person to make the decisions will vary depending on the context. Sometimes you will be the one who will have to make a decision. Sometimes you should delegate and let one of the team members decide, or even the full team. You may also be required to bring it to the sponsor or governance committee of the project.

In all cases, decisions are required to have a successful project. Make good decisions. Take action with clarity and speed. Don't be tentative, insecure, or relying indefinitely on others or on consensus. There is a cost to making bad decisions, but there is also a cost of indecision. Worrying about hypothetical consequences hinders progress.

Be the leader, and ensure that strategic decisions are made. Then ensure that the decisions are followed by actions.

This is a key part of project success. This is a fundamental trait of being a strategic project leader.

CHAPTER 17

Conclusion

Not a conclusion but a journey

We have covered the subject of leadership in project management broadly in this book. Many of the topics covered could be the subject of a book of their own, but I hope this book has given you enough material to guide your reflections on the subject. I hope it inspired you to take actions, learn, and further enhance your leadership skills.

Developing our leadership skills is not a process with a defined start and end. It is not a checklist to be completed. Nobody can claim to have fully mastered leadership. As such, it is not a learning process. Learning leadership is a journey, more complicated than learning a complex but well-defined process. It does not have a definitive answer like a mathematical formula; it is a life journey. You can start the journey, but there is no end to the exploration of leadership.

The journey in this book covered many topics. It started first with establishing a solid foundation. The next step was a view of the leader as a human, as developing this view is also an exercise in personal development. Self-awareness is an essential step to support personal development and professional skills such as leadership. We then covered other topics such as values and ethics, team management, strategic thinking, and decision-making.

Leadership is a necessary skill to manage strategic projects and optimize results in a dynamic world. Our current world is in constant evolution, and supervising tasks is often no longer sufficient. Leadership skills are required to navigate the various uncertainties of a project.

A story

While working on this book, I had the chance to live a unique experience. On a Saturday morning, my family and I went skiing, like we do during most of the winter. After all, if we are going to suffer the strength of the Canadian winter, we may as well enjoy it as much as possible, and skiing is an outdoor activity the four of us like to do. The mountain, the slope, the chairlift; we all love downhill skiing.

Our two sons were with their ski instructor, and I was skiing with my wife. As does happen from time to time, the chairlift stopped on our way up. This usually lasts only a few seconds, or at worst a few minutes. Often it is caused by a beginner who missed his entry onto or exit off the chair.

This time, nothing. Time passed by, and we had two attempts to make the chairlift work again. We moved ahead a few meters but then stopped again. Staff advised us after about thirty minutes that it should be working again in ten minutes. After another twenty minutes of waiting, we were finally informed that they would have to evacuate the skiers manually.

This was a long process. It was -13 C (or 9 F), and -25 C (or -13 F) with the wind chill factor. We could see our kids with the ski instructor about twelve chairs ahead, higher on the chairlift. We could not do anything for them and could only hope that they were fine.

With nothing to do, all we could do was wait and manage our own emotions, keeping our hopes high that it would be resolved soon, and trust others.

My wife was able to obtain information on our children's health through a young man working with the ski patrol. He ran to their chair and talked to them, reassured them, and came back to us.

When they finally rescued us, the process required collaboration. It was important that both my wife and I jump on the platform at the same time.

This is like the life of a project manager in a dynamic and changing environment. It is impossible to control everything. You have to delegate and trust others. Collaboration is essential. Communication can help resolve issues, and it is important to find a method of communication adapted to the context and the problem.

In the end, we were all safe. The staff at the ski resort took care of us very well. For our kids, it was almost like an adventure, something unique that very few have done.

Life is full of uncertainties. The tools and techniques of project management let you handle the predictable parts of the project, but leadership is important to navigate the unusual events of life. It is impossible to avoid all problems, and even if it were possible, it would result in a life without opportunities.

After that ski adventure, what do we do the next weekend? We went skiing again. We made sure we had sufficiently warm clothes, because one never knows what can happen, but we did go back.

Life is too short to be paralyzed and afraid.

Be the leader

Your projects need a leader, so be the leader of your project. This will enhance opportunities and success in your career.

One of the best ways to continue this journey is to join a forum on the Internet and participate in discussions. You can also find books, podcasts, and websites providing information on the subject. It is a fascinating journey, with each step bringing new discoveries. The best leadership development will even impact positively your personal life, relationships with your spouse and kids, and other personal interests.

Appendix

Bonus

You can find a resource page for this book on my website. The page includes links relevant to this book, along with some bonus materials with other products or services relevant to project management.

http://www.project-aria.ca/leadership-toolbox-project-managers-resources/

On the resources page, there is a contact form if you wish to contact me directly.

I hope you enjoyed reading this book. If you enjoyed it and found it useful, I'd be grateful if you would post a review on Amazon. Your support does make a difference. I read all the reviews personally, and they provide a wealth of information. Your feedback will be used to make this book even better, and to create other books or products in the future.

Thank you again for reading the book.

Connect with Project-Aria

Thank you so much for taking the time to read this book. I'm honored by the time you gave me. I hope this book inspires you to advance farther in your career on the path of project leadership. There is an interesting world of opportunities, successes, and achievements for those who are ready to expand beyond the role of managing tasks.

You can connect with me at the following sites:

Website

The home of Project-Aria can be accessed at the address below. You can also subscribe to the RSS feed to receive the latest posts, or to the mailing list.

http://www.project-aria.ca

Mailing List

If you have not already done so, subscribe to our mailing list to get the latest information delivered directly to your inbox. You will also receive special articles that we only send to our subscribers.

After registration, please don't forget to complete the registration process by clicking on the link in the confirmation email you will receive in your inbox.

http://www.project-aria.ca/subscribe

Facebook Page

Project-Aria has a Facebook Page. Please visit us and like our page to follow our publications.

https://www.facebook.com/project.aria.ca

Twitter

Project-Aria is very active on Twitter. Follow our account to get interesting information on project management, leadership, and productivity.

https://twitter.com/PMProjectAria

Google+ Page

Google+ has many active thought leaders on project management. Project-Aria also has a Google+ Page and engages in discussion with others on leadership and project management.

https://plus.google.com/+Project-ariaCa/posts

Google+ Community

To discuss project management further, join the Project-Aria Google+ community:

https://plus.google.com/communities/1109032124189226 96779

About the author

Michel Dion is a Project Management Professional (PMP). He is the founder and developer of the website Project-Aria, a site dedicated to project management with a focus on achieving better results in a dynamic world. You can find various articles on project management, leadership, productivity, career and training, and also covering the mind and health of the project manager on his website. He has been active in various online project management communities since July 2012.

Michel has a diverse background. He is a professional accountant, CPA-CGA in Canada. He also has a certification in Internal Audit (CIA), Risk Management (CRMA), and Fraud (CFE). Michel has managed many projects in his career, including special initiatives and emergency projects. He lives in Ottawa, Ontario, Canada, with his wife Valérie and two sons, Tristan and Mathias. He enjoys skiing with his family but easily admits to being more of a summer guy. As he says, there are no days too hot for him (even in the Caribbean).

Among other things, he also has interests in music (his first bachelor degree is in classical music), chess, fitness, travel, photography, and technology. He has loved technology since the moment he first played on the TRS80. Despite that, his two sons insist that they know more about technology than him. He is also interested in languages, with the goal of mastering four languages. He is fluently bilingual (English and French) and is currently learning Spanish and Swedish.

Michel likes to learn and discover new things, and he has a passion for sharing his knowledge and coaching others, which has led him to develop his website, participate in numerous online groups and communities, and write books.

Other books by Michel Dion

Project Leadership - Lessons from 40 PPM Experts on Making the Transition from Project Management to Project Leadership

Participation as an author in this compilation of 40 articles on project leadership, prepared by Studio B Productions, Inc. and sponsored by AtTask, now called Workfront. The book is available on Slideshare.

http://www.slideshare.net/DavidRogelberg/project-mgmt-finalattask2

http://www.studiob.com/

http://www.workfront.com/resources/ebook/lessons-from-40-ppm-experts/

www.ingramcontent.com/pod-product-compliance
Lightning Source LLC
Chambersburg PA
CBHW070928210326
41520CB00021B/6850